Expressions of Judgment

Expressions of Judgment

An Essay on Kant's Aesthetics

Eli Friedlander

Harvard University Press

Cambridge, Massachusetts, & London, England
2015

First printing

Library of Congress Cataloging-in-Publication Data

Friedlander, Eli.
   Expressions of judgment : an essay on Kant's aesthetics / Eli Friedlander.
      pages   cm
   Includes bibliographical references and index.
   ISBN 978-0-674-36820-0 (alk. paper)
      1. Kant, Immanuel, 1724–1804. Kritik der Urteilskraft.   2. Judgment
(Aesthetics)   3. Aesthetics.   I. Title.
   B2784.F75   2014
   121—dc23   2014006412

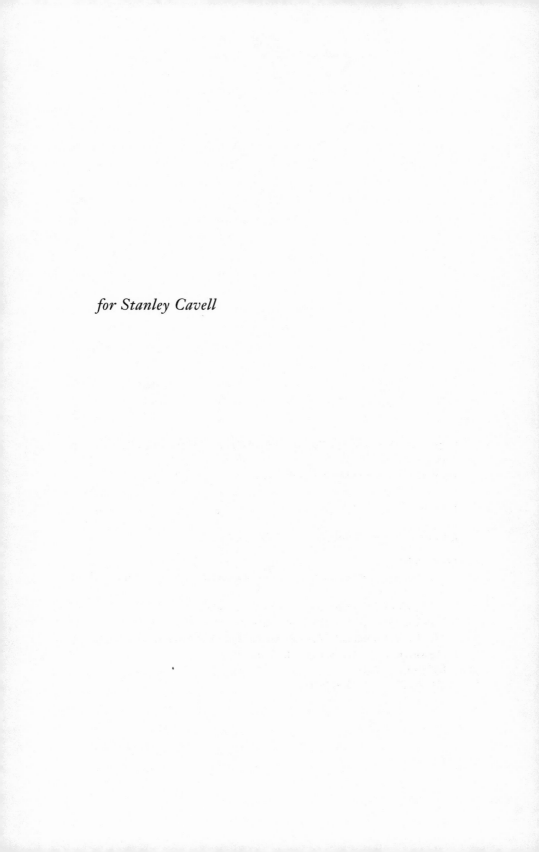

for Stanley Cavell

Contents

Preface and Acknowledgments

The present book was written gradually over a period of more than twenty years of teaching Kant's *Critique of Judgment* in classes at different levels. It has therefore something of the character of an introduction to Kant's aesthetics. Yet, not every work of philosophy can be introduced equally well, that is, without compromising one's sense of its rigor and complexity. What made this possible in the case of the 'Third Critique' is, as I came to realize, that work's own unified character. It allowed the bringing together of didactic aspirations with the ambition to illuminate and engage the depths of Kant's work.

The following chapters are, therefore, not so much an attempt to simplify the 'Third Critique' so as to make it easily accessible but rather an effort to remain true to a dimension of simplicity inherent in the work itself. Call this the simplicity of the systematic. As will become evident, the 'Third Critique' is a work of enormous richness, but the wealth of themes, issues, and distinctions unfolds with an inner movement or inner life to which it is imperative to remain attuned.

Such a sense of unity is not easily conveyed. It cannot be represented as various contents might be given, nor is it captured in a line of argument;

rather, it is a matter of going through the work in a certain way. It must be expressed by bringing together its themes, relating concerns that are often separated in the successive order of the text. So as to engage the *Critique of Judgment* with that task in mind, I found it necessary at times to recast Kant's language, not thereby insinuating that his formulations are unclear but rather giving up on his mode of expression for the sake of my effort to show how the material belongs together. The result is therefore different from more scholarly books on Kant's *Critique of Judgment*, although from beginning to end it will equally be devoted to explicating that work. The freedom I allowed myself in reformulating Kant's position has a cost but hopefully also brings a benefit that is much harder to achieve by other means.

In order to maintain a pace of exposition suited to make the unity of Kant's text perspicuous, I have chosen not to explicitly engage the body of writings devoted to Kant's oeuvre. If I were to single out one issue in which the present interpretation differs most clearly from other approaches to the *Critique of Judgment*, I would emphasize the inner connection formed between the aesthetic judgment and meaning or expression (thus the title of my book, *Expressions of Judgment*). No doubt it is often noted that for Kant beauty is meaningful as, for example, when he conceives of beauty as a symbol of morality. And yet that general analogy between the aesthetic phenomenon and the sphere of morality is, to my mind, only part of the story. Indeed, what is at stake is the meaning found in the particular experience of beauty, most clearly evident in being responsive to works of art.

By emphasizing the dimension of meaning in the aesthetic judgment, I want to counter the still common view that, in the face of beauty, we have a certain feeling of pleasure, which is the visible symptom of our faculties doing some work, less than consciously, inside. The pleasure is one that, on this view, we would identify somehow as being of the right kind (say, realizing by introspection that we have no interest in the object), and we would thereby be justified in making the judgment "This is beautiful." True enough, it is not uncommon to feel wordless in the face of beauty. Beauty demands a response, and we might often find our answers faint or our words quite inadequate, falling short of our experience. But this very lack is a mode of inhabitation of language; it points at the unfulfilled demand to make one's encounter with beauty intelligible. Far from drawing apart language and feeling such wordlessness shows their intimate proximity. We should not take our sometimes inarticulate reactions to beauty as a standard for what a judgment of taste is as such.

The force of Kant's *Critique of Judgment* can become apparent not only in engaging its sheer depth and complexity but also in recognizing its pertinence to the highest creative endeavors. It is not just that the *Critique of Judgment* had an immediate influence on some of Kant's contemporaries, such as Schiller and Goethe. Rather, as I will try to indicate, in the albeit too few and too sketchy remarks interspersed in notes, the significance of artistic and critical endeavors of romanticism and modernism can be illuminated by way of Kant's work. The presence of deep affinities between Kant's philosophy and artistic as well as critical practices extending to our present day is surprising to the extent that there is no detailed discussion of art works in the 'Third Critique.' The few examples Kant does provide leave the impression that he had limited acquaintance with art. It is as though Kant is sensitive to the dimensions of aesthetic experience by following the implications of his systematic thinking. But this itself is highly significant. Kant, one might say, reaches the essence of the beautiful by taking his *philosophy* to the limit, opening thereby a view onto the kinship of beauty and truth.

Over the years, I have had the privilege of conversations on Kant and aesthetics with friends, colleagues, and students (these being by no means categories excluding one another). I am particularly indebted to Amichai Amit, Yoav Beirach, James Conant, Ilit Ferber, Paul Franks, Gideon Freudenthal, Ido Geiger, Hannah Ginsborg, Moran Godess-Riccitelli, Keren Gorodeisky, Michal Grover-Friedlander, Arata Hamawaki, Hagi Kenaan, Irad Kimhi, Yakir Levine, David MacArthur, Nimrod Matan, Noa Merkin, Ofra Rechter, Aviv Reiter, Ori Rotlevy, Yaron Senderowicz, Pioter Shmugliakov, David Wellbery, and Johnathan Wertheim Soen.

The material of this book was taught recently in a seminar of the Kant program at Tel Aviv and Ben-Gurion Universities. I am grateful to the participants, faculty and students, for their comments and questions. Portions of the chapters were also presented at the the Sawyer Seminar on the Problem of Non-Discursive Thought at the University of Chicago, as well as during my visits and lectures at the Johns Hopkins Humanities

Center; I have greatly benefited from the responses and the conversations that ensued. Lindsay Waters, my editor at Harvard University Press, was a generous interlocutor, as I shared with him my thoughts on Kant over the years. He was supportive, encouraging, and patient despite the many transformations that the project went through. I also thank the anonymous readers he chose to review the manuscript, for their extremely helpful comments.

I am grateful to the Israel Science Foundation for the grant I received to complete the writing of this book. My thanks also go to John Donohue and Carol Hoke for editing the manuscript, as well as to Sarale Ben Asher, who assisted me with the final stages of readying the work for publication.

Stanley Cavell advised my first attempts to write on Kant's *Critique of Judgment*. His influence extends far beyond the dissertation I wrote with him at Harvard. The impact of conversations we have had and the inspiration of his writings has remained with me through the years of working on the subject. I dedicate the book to him.

Expressions of Judgment

Introduction

Before entering into the intricacies of Kant's *Critique of Judgment*, I wish in this introduction to provide some background for it in Kant's Critical Philosophy. In the first section I summarize central points in the account of judgment in the *Critique of Pure Reason*, and in the second section I sketch in very broad lines the systematic horizon in which Kant's treatment of aesthetics finds its place.

§1. Judgment: General and Transcendental

Neither beauty nor art, neither pleasure nor creativity, but rather judgment is the fundamental notion of Kant's treatment of aesthetics. The latter forms the first part of a critique of *the power of judgment*. While the aesthetic might offer a field for the capacity to judge to most purely manifest itself, it is important to keep in mind that judgment plays a role in all uses of our higher faculties.

In his account of cognition, Kant introduces the capacity to judge to account for the *application* of our general concepts to particular cases: "If the understanding in general is explained as the faculty of rules, then the power of judgment is the faculty of *subsuming* under rules, i.e. of determining whether something stands under a given rule . . . or not"[1] (A132/B171). Though it bears on every domain of objects whatsoever, the inquiry into the principles for putting that capacity to use is nevertheless not part of logic. The proper employment of judgment cannot be captured by general rules. Were we to conceive of general rules for the exercise of the very capacity to apply rules, a vicious regress would ensue. Given any such set of rules, we could always raise the question of when it is appropriate to apply *them* and thus would need a further rule for settling that matter.[2] There is no way to account *in general* for how to subsume the particular under the universal. The gap between them cannot be filled by an appeal to a procedure that would be valid for all cases. That is, the problem of application cannot be resolved generally, irrespective of the kind of concepts applied and the specific diversity of the world.

Put slightly differently, judgment is not a matter of knowledge of abstract rules but rather constitutes a capacity that must be *exercised*: ". . . and so it becomes clear that although the understanding is certainly capable of being instructed and equipped through rules, the power of judgment is a special talent that cannot be taught but only practiced *(geübt)*" (A133/B172). Kant gives several intuitive examples in which we would wish to distinguish a person who merely has the knowledge of rules in theory and the one who can be credited with exercising judgment in applying them to concrete cases: "A physician, therefore, a judge, or a statesman, can have many fine pathological, juridical, or political rules in his head, of which he can even be a thorough teacher, and yet can easily stumble in their application, either because he is lacking in natural power of judgment (though not in understanding), and to be sure understands the universal *in abstracto* but cannot distinguish whether a case *in concreto* belongs under it, or also because he has not received adequate training for this judgment through examples and actual business" (A134/B173).[3] Even given an excellent code of law, a judge would need to exercise judgment to decide which law is pertinent for the specific case at hand. (Should this death be counted as murder, manslaughter, or accidental?) A code of law must have generality; its rules are just that—they are rules—they must go beyond the plurality of cases, and their application, or extension to a new case, is not automatic, algorithmic, or itself rule governed. And even if an experienced physician might gather guidelines or maxims of judgment, sum up his *use* of medical expertise, such maxims would be different from those a judge might come up with out of his experience of the cases prosecuted in his court. The more judgment is exercised, the more it is sensitive to the particular character of the field in which it is put to use.

The difference Kant points to between acquiring theoretical knowledge on the one hand and practicing or gaining experience by conducting "actual business" on the other is clarified further by being aligned with the distinction between what can be *learned* and what demands *talent*. What we can receive from others and can further impart to others must be able to be articulated in rules that could in principle be followed by anyone. Talent, on the other hand, is what we have from nature (even if it is manifest in matters that are not natural). Talent is not something that everyone has. It is not distributed evenly by nature. Kant then surprisingly appeals to talent in relation to the exercise of one of our rational capacities (albeit when it is put to use in applying empirical concepts). This kind of natural ground is further characterized by Kant as "mother wit" *(Mutterwitz)*, "the lack of which cannot be made good by any school; for although such a school can provide a limited understanding with plenty of rules borrowed from the insight of others and as it were graft these onto it, nevertheless the faculty for making use of them correctly must belong to the student himself, and in the absence of such a natural gift no rule that one might prescribe to him for this aim is safe from misuse" (A133/B172).

Even though the independent exercise of the capacity to judge is a matter of talent, and cannot be learned, it must nevertheless be awakened: "This is also the sole and great utility of examples: that they sharpen the power of judgment" (A134/B173).[4] An example is a particular case of a rule or concept. In teaching by way of examples we start with the particular in order to lead to the understanding of the universal or the rule. The example must be such that the character of the rule is particularly well manifest in it. Thus one has to choose carefully one's examples when trying to teach a rule or a concept to someone who does not know it. If, for instance, I want to explain what a prime number is, I will take as an example the number 5 or 7 rather than a six-digit prime number. "Thus examples are the leading-strings *(Gängelwagen)* of the power of judgment, which he who lacks the natural talent for judgment can never do without" (A134/B173). Those who lack talent for judging will always depend on further examples, just like children learning to walk need constant support.

In broaching the problem of judgment in the *Critique of Pure Reason*, Kant thus mainly puts aside, as falling outside the scope of a strict philosophical treatment, a variety of questions associated with judgment which his introduction has raised: What is it to judge in the absence of rules? What is it to have a good sense of the intricacies of the particular? Why is judgment a capacity that must essentially be exercised, and how is it refined with actual experience? What is the relation of judgment to natural talent, and can there be universality in a field in which talent matters? Can the role of the particular in teaching and learning be thematized? And is there a way to account systematically for exemplification? These questions will be answered as judgment receives a critical elaboration in the *Critique of Judgment*. They point to central dimensions of the field of aesthetic judgment.

Kant's discussion of judgment in the 'Analytic of Principles' in the *Critique of Pure Reason* has two sides. In the first place it emphasizes how problematic it is to provide a systematic philosophical articulation of the power of judgment insofar as we think of it in general, regardless of the kind of concepts we employ. In the second place, these considerations set the stage for the specificity of the issue of *transcendental* judgment, of the problem of the application of the pure concepts of the understanding, the *categories*, to the manifold of intuition.[5] It is with respect to the possibility of this latter deployment of judgment that Kant is committed to give a complete a priori systematic justification.

We can briefly characterize the specific problem in the application of the categories by noting that in their case judgment is viewed not only as bringing together general and particular but also as serving as an intermediate link between essentially different *kinds* of representation, namely concepts and intuitions. Concepts are essentially mediate representations of an object, general rules that are the product of the understanding for unifying the manifold of the given. Intuitions are singular and immediate representations given to us in sensibility. With empirical concepts such as "dog," we might not be aware of the problem in bringing together such distinct representations since the concept itself might have been drawn from repeated experience of particular cases, sharing some intuitively recognizable traits. But the problem is acute with the categories, the pure products of our intellect, which *in principle* have nothing in common with the given manifold of intuition they must unify. Yet, as Kant writes: "in all subsumptions of an object under a concept the representations of the object must be *homogeneous* with the concept" (A137/B176).

It is to resolve this difficulty that Kant invokes, in the case of the transcendental judgment, a mediating element which shares features of the two sides it brings together and is produced by a faculty that itself can be thought to stand between the activity of the understanding and the passivity of intuition, namely the imagination. The imagination shares with the understanding its active capacity to produce from itself representations, but its material is intuitive. The imagination does not think but produces images. The products of the imagination that allow the application of the categories to intuition are not rules. That is, Kant does not retract in the transcendental case the claim made about judgment in general, that it has no rules. For what the imagination provides are schemata. Schemata share with rules their generality and share with the particular an intuitive character.

In order to suggest what such schemata of the categories could be, note that the hybrid capacity of the imagination has an intimate relation to time. It provides, in its empirical use, a way to go beyond what is immediately given in perception. It produces visions of the future as well as retrieves memories of the past. In the transcendental case, the schemata the imagination produced to bridge between categories and intuitions are indeed pure and have no empirical basis. They are mere image-schemes of the form time takes in the realization of each category. They are pure constructions in inner sense, constructions in and of time. Not wanting to say more about this complex and notoriously obscure matter of the schematism, let us merely retain in mind the connection Kant forms between judgment, the imagination, and a sense of time, for it will become central in considering the field of the aesthetic.

§2. The Dimensions of Mediation

a. Completion as Mediation

To read the *Critique of Judgment* so as to capture its inner unity requires moving between two perspectives: first, attentively elucidating the inner articulations of the grammar of the aesthetic judgment so as to make evident that Kant captures central aspects of our *experience* of beauty (and sublimity). But it is no less important, second, to conceive the field of judgment in terms of its systematic place in Kant's critical philosophy. In particular, this requires asking about the relation of the aesthetic to cognition on the one hand and to morality on the other. It also requires asking how Kant positions the 'Third Critique' as *the completion* of the critical enterprise. Whereas the doctrinal part of philosophy may remain open, completion is *essential* to the validity of the critical part of philosophy. For, "critique . . . is the propaedeutic of all philosophy" (5:194), and it must constitute the framework within which philosophy can at all be conducted in a scientific fashion as doctrine or as metaphysics.

Yet the mode of completion of the critical part by way of a critique of *judgment* is problematized by Kant's insistence that judgment has no realm of objects over which it is legislative. Strictly speaking, there are only two realms of philosophy in which reason can exercise its dominion, in which it is involved in the lawful constitution of a domain of objects, thus in which there is room for a metaphysics, for further doctrinal work: nature and freedom, the conditioned and the unconditioned, the realm of knowledge and that of the will. There is a metaphysics of nature and a metaphysics of morals, but no doctrinary part following upon the critique of judgment. So why is a critique of the power of judgment necessary at all?

The *Critique of Judgment* completes the critical enterprise by providing the framework or blueprint for undertaking the task of bridging between the two realms of cognition and morals. The mediating function of judgment is thus broadened from its initial thematization in the 'First Critique.' Not only does it mediate the general and the particular, allowing the application of rules. Nor is it just mediating between intuition and concept by way of the imagination. It is now also given the role of mediating between the realms opened by the two first Critiques, of constituting a bridge between nature and freedom. *Purposiveness* is the central notion that brings together our experience and knowledge of nature with the practical determinations of the will and the realm of freedom. The notion of purpose undoubtedly has a central role in laying out the structure of the domain of action (even though with pure practical reason, the purpose is subordinated to duty, the good to the right). But in the 'Third Critique' purposiveness is dissociated from the will and introduced into experience itself. It comes to characterize on the one hand the experience of the natural world—in our teleological judgments and on the other, our most natural responses, namely the pleasure and pain in our aesthetic judgments.

b. The Horizon of Mediation

The three Critiques form a systematic unity in which all the needs of reason can find a place to be addressed. Indeed, since a critique of reason essentially is reason's own self-criticism, it not only draws the bounds of its proper uses but also must find a place to realize the needs whose satisfaction was denied to reason in its improper use. This systematic unity can, in part, be characterized by a structure of deferment. The *Critique of Pure Reason* limits our knowledge to the conditioned. But Kant doesn't simply deny satisfaction to our claims to absolute knowledge; he also shows that there is truth to reason's drive for the unconditioned. He shows a way for its fulfillment in a different domain, namely as an unconditional principle of the will. Similarly one might argue that the *Critique of Practical Reason* places limits on conditioned practical reason and its end, happiness. Yet, once more the human need for happiness is not dismissed even though in its reasonable articulation it must be absolutely subordinate to being worthy of happiness.

Where could that reasonable need for happiness receive any satisfaction? What would count as *reason* taking this need into account? Here, it would seem, the possibility of satisfaction is infinitely deferred and identified with the way nature and reason are brought together in what Kant calls "the highest good." The harmonization of reason and nature in the highest good is the ideal of a world in which happiness is proportional to goodness. Importantly, although it is up to human beings to lead a moral life, it is not in their power to apportion the happiness they may be worthy of appropriately. In Kant's moral philosophy the ideal of the highest good goes hand in hand with the postulates of practical faith: freedom, the existence of God, and the immortality of the soul.

Even if it is not in our power to realize the highest good but can only hope for it, it would be reasonable to seek in the world a foothold for that hope of the harmonization of nature and our rational capacities. For such hope to be sustainable there must be a sign of that possible harmony in the world, here and now. It is indeed part of the grammar of hope that its fulfillment cannot be guaranteed, but it is just as much part of it that we can find signs to awaken it. The 'Third Critique' takes the aesthetic to be a field in which we are given such indication. Quoting Stendhal one could say that for Kant "beauty is only a promise of happiness" (which is to be distinguished from finding happiness in beauty; the latter would make the aesthetic into a mere substitute, and amount to the aestheticization of human life).

c. Mediation and Systematicity

Philosophy must not only answer all the fundamental needs of reason but also do so in a systematic way. The unity presupposed in the very idea of a critique demands that systematic interconnection of all the questions of philosophy. Reason must be able to take care of itself and can depend on nothing external to it to resolve its inner tensions. In the *Critique of Pure Reason*, Kant characterizes the systematicity to which reason strives for as purposive: "This highest formal unity, which rests solely on concepts of reason, is the *purposive* unity of things" (A686/B714).

The 'Third Critique' translates reason's demand for systematicity into a principle that guides judgment. This principle guides our inquiry into nature and justifies our teleological judgments. Yet, there is clearly also an aesthetic dimension to systematicity, revealed in feeling, a subjective dimension that might even underlie the objective idea of the system. This aesthetic dimension of systematicity can be explicated in terms of the notion of mediation. Systematic mediation implies taking everything into account, balancing various sides, various needs, or various demands. But it is manifest in its purity only when there is no prior standard for the ordering in balance of the different sides. Put differently, systematicity brings together different domains into a unity without reducing the principles of the one to those of another. It is thus essentially different from a hierarchical ordering based on first principles. Keeping balanced the various manifestation of reason is a matter that requires a sense of judgment.

We can also say that to encompass the critical enterprise, reason must thematize its *sense* of its own inner unity. To put the matter cautiously, there will be *analogies* between reason's capacity to sense the balance of all its aspects and the form of aesthetic judgment. The role of reason as the ultimate judge that balances together all of man's needs and orients itself by feeling this balance is best figured not by our cognitive or moral natures but in the aesthetic. The aesthetic is, in that respect, a training ground for philosophy's highest aspirations.[6]

d. Mediation and the Idea of the Human

In the 'Transcendental Doctrine of Method' of the *Critique of Pure Reason*, Kant divides the domain of philosophy by way of three fundamental questions: "What can I know?" "What ought I to do?" and "What can I hope for?" The 'First Critique' and the 'Second Critique' answer respectively the first and second questions, and it would seem that the third question was intended by Kant to be answered by a philosophical investigation of religion. This hardly leaves room for the critical investigation of the aesthetic. Granted, when writing the *Critique of Pure Reason*, Kant did not envisage aesthetics as falling within the scope of philosophy.[7] But where is it to be placed, in the space of these questions, after he realizes its importance for the Critical philosophy? Is there a specific question for which the investigation of the aesthetic provides an answer? Or is judgment related, as I suggested earlier, to the problem of the concrete coordination of the independent answers?

In his 'Lectures on Logic,' Kant sums up the systematic interconnection of the three questions of philosophy by way of the question "What is man?" This would point to philosophical anthropology as the field in which the different needs of reason come together in being applied to the embodied existence of man. The investigation of the aesthetic can in many ways be seen as the critical framework for such coordinated application. Relating the aesthetic to the question "What is man?" one might want to recall how beauty is a uniquely human phenomenon. According to Kant the moral law is valid for all rational beings, but "beauty has purport and significance only for human beings, i.e. for beings at once animal and rational (but not merely for them as rational—intelligent beings—but only for them as at once animal and rational)" (5:210). The specific appeal of beauty to the human can be explained initially, in terms of a certain equality in the involvement of the various faculties, as though all the capacities of a human being must take part and be harmonized in that experience. That is, in the moral domain there is an absolute predominance of reason. Insofar as other faculties take part in characterizing that domain, it would be by serving reason. Similarly, cognition is where the understanding rules or gives the law. Imagination, or even reason, serves the understanding's realization of its capacity. But in the aesthetic our faculties have equal shares. Even if reason is sometimes less prominent (say, in beauty), this will be balanced by its centrality in the experience of the sublime. Moreover, the aesthetic can even give a higher place, an equal footing, to what seems in other contexts to be too natural or contingent a product of our bodily existence, namely to pleasure. The aesthetic appeals to the human being as a whole insofar as it is a field that brings together all of that being's higher capacities to work or, should one say play, together.

e. Mediation, Duality, and Analogy

In Mediation a bridge is constructed between two wholly distinct realms, a medium established sharing characteristics of the two antithetic sides. One can easily underestimate the implications of this claim by taking Kant's characterization of the task of constructing a bridge between nature and freedom to be a mere figure for what is in any case an endless task. What would be more correct to say is that a dimension of figuration or analogy becomes integral to our significant experience of the world. It would be yet another way to point to the central role provided to the imagination in this third Critique.

One might start to appreciate the extent of the involvement of the imagination if we consider that an analogical transposition, a simile, is required to state the fundamental principle of reflective judgment on nature: ". . . by this concept nature is represented *as if* an understanding contained the ground of the unity of the manifold of its empirical laws . . . this concept is entirely different from practical finality (in human art or even morals), though it is doubtless thought after this analogy" (5:180, my emphasis). Analogy, the 'as if,' appears also in other parts of the 'Third Critique,' thus "nature proved beautiful when it wore the appearance of art; and art can only be termed beautiful, where we are conscious of its being art, while yet it has the appearance of nature" (5:306). And one of the most famous moments in the 'Third Critique' is the analogical relation formed between beauty and morality when beauty is called the "symbol of morality."[8]

The appearance of such transpositions or analogical bringing together of two domains at crucial junctures in the work is an upshot of the mediating function of judgment. Indeed at least in the case of the aesthetic one cannot assume that the space of mediation objectively exists for us to cross. Rather it must be opened by involving our imagination without having any prior rule to guarantee its proper use. This raises the question: Would the free involvement of the imagination in the possibility of mediation inherently problematize its validity? Or can the task of judgment itself open the prospects of another truthfulness at the heart of the aesthetic "as if"?

The precise structure of mediation, as it is exhibited in the field of the aesthetic judgment, is something to be developed throughout this book, but from the general understanding of this task of judgment it is possible to draw methodological guidelines so as to orient the reading of the text. Bridging is not only an overarching figure but rather, I would argue, is at work in each and every aspect of the 'Third Critique,' apparent in the splits and divisions that characterize the field of judgment. Mediation is always between sides, so that its field will not be such as to present a unitary character. Nor would we speak of simple dichotomies, but rather of a field characterized by dualities. Such duality is already evident in the very form of that book, starting from the fact that, contrary to Kant's other works, which are organized around the principles of one particular realm, it is divided into two separate parts—the aesthetic and the teleological. Of course, Kant relates those two domains to features of judgment as such, taking the aesthetic to be making manifest the subjective aspect of judgment and the teleological its objective aspect. But to provide that explanation only begs the question, namely why is it that, with judgment, each of those two sides, the subjective and the objective, gets a field of its own. The more one investigates the nature of judgment, the more those dualities characteristic of mediation will appear to structure its proper field of application. Indeed the 'Critique of Aesthetic Judgment' will be traversed by such dualities at various levels: the beautiful and the sublime, free and dependent beauty, ideal beauty and the pure judgment of taste, the genius and the judge of taste, natural beauty and art. There will also appear new forms of relating and separating subject and object, the objective and the subjective, cognition and will, the natural and the artificial, intuition and concept, experience and idea, singular and universal as well as the individual and the common. The necessity to think in terms of dualities is specifically addressed in Part III of my book, in which I treat of the different ways to hold together nature and art, as well as in Part IV, by the special attention I give to extreme limit cases in which, I argue, the beautiful touches upon the sublime.

Part I

The Analytic of the Beautiful

For the true critic, the actual *judgment* is the ultimate step—something that comes after everything else, never the basis of his activities. In the ideal case, he forgets to pass judgment.

—Walter Benjamin

Kant divides the 'Analytic of the Beautiful' into four moments according to the headings of the table of the categories: Quality, Quantity, Relation, and Modality.[1] Each of the four moments is summed up in a formulation involving negation: Taste estimates an object *apart from any interest*, the beautiful pleases *apart from a concept* universally, it is the form of finality in an object *apart from the representation of an end*, and it is that which, *apart from a concept*, is cognized as an object of a necessary delight. Before proceeding any further, it might be advisable to consider those two structural matters which frame Kant's discussion. For they are liable to produce a picture that would from the start lead us astray. Given Kant's reliance on the table of categories one might be tempted to model the aesthetic judgment on a cognitive judgment. The negative formulation might further suggest that it would be less than a full-fledged cognition, lacking some of its central characteristics, in particular any use of concepts. We would then start off attributing to Kant what might be called a *minimalist* view of the aesthetic judgment, taking it to be a deficient mode of the conceptual articulation of experience exhibited in cognition.

To be sure, the negative characterization of the four moments of the 'Analytic' establishes a dependence of that which is introduced and eluci-dated, namely the aesthetic judgment upon beauty, on that which is negated. But it does not make aesthetic judgment into a lesser state of mind. It is as though the grammar of the aesthetic judgment cannot be illuminated di-rectly but rather always against better-recognized modes of thought by way of similarities *and* differences. For that reason, it is always important to keep in mind that Kant frames his discussion not only against the back-ground of cognition but also at the same time against characteristics in-volving the faculty of desire (such as purpose or interest). The aesthetic will turn out to be similar *both* to cognition and to desire and therefore will be different from each. That there are no fully independent characterizations of the field of the beautiful is, one might conjecture, the upshot of the mediating role of judgment. The field of mediation is opened only in terms of the sides it brings together.

Similarly, Kant's assertion that taste estimates "apart from a concept" implies a retreat from our objective modes of relating to the world in cog-nition and morality. But this need not be taken to dissociate the aesthetic judgment from meaning, nor does it make it a mute pleasurable response to an object. We might forego our active reasoned engagement with the world, but only in order to open the way for a richer, more natural, or more *significant* intimacy with that which is judged. Thus avoiding the repre-sentation of the object to ourselves by way of an independently determined concept need not preclude other ways of engaging our conceptual capacity in its experience. The release from predetermined modes of approaching the object might indeed allow us to realize to the utmost the potential of our representational capacities.

§1. The First Moment

"The judgment of taste is aesthetic," writes Kant in the heading of the first section of the first moment of the 'Analytic of the Beautiful.' The criterion of our estimation of beauty is the feeling of pleasure. But how can a mere feeling validate a judgment? Take Kant's general characteriza-tion of judgment as "the faculty for thinking the particular as contained

in the universal" (5:179). In the simplest case, a judgment attributes a concept to a particular and exhibits their unity in a determinate state of affairs
(for example, "the table is round"). That unity is manifested by grasping
the object in a certain way, as this *kind* of thing, that is, through the concept we chose to represent it to ourselves. In so doing a direction is given
to one's approach to the object; it is determined from a certain perspective.
There are many other such perspectives (rather than the roundness of the
table one could consider it as wooden, tall, brown etc.). Thus through the
determination of the concept in the judgment about an object, a certain
aspect of the thing becomes prominent, and the manifold multiplicity of
the particular, while not disappearing, recedes to the background.

Now the validity of the judgment depends on whether in fact the object
has the property in question. The fundamental issue is correctness or truth,
and not pleasure. Agreeableness doesn't enter into the determination of the
agreement of judgment and reality. We might try to introduce an affective
dimension to judgment by noting that judgments are guided by interests.
In other words, we mostly judge things to be so and so not for judging's
sake but because we have certain interests in ascertaining the situation in a
certain way ("Here is a round table! Exactly what we need," exclaims King
Arthur). The directedness of assertions is related to the interests involved
in making them. But the interest is, even if not wholly external, then at least
partial to that which is judged. Interestedness, most significantly, then subordinates our experience to a particular perspective. Even if this introduces pleasure and displeasure into our judgments through the satisfaction
of these interests, it does so by subordinating the judgment to external
purposes, to what is deemed good by the faculty of desire.

Thus, in trying to account for the possibility of an aesthetic judgment,
of pleasure and displeasure being *intrinsically* related to the exercise of
judgment, we have a double problem: How are we to think of judgment
apart from the criterion of truth as the accordance of the judgment with a
state of affairs? And how are we to have pleasure in judging without relating to desire, that is, without relying on prior interests that direct us to the
object? Establishing judgment on neither truth, nor goodness, but rather
pleasure demands that we reconceive the relation between the two poles
of universal and particular, of concept and object. The act of judgment need

not be conceived only as ascertaining that the particular object falls under a given concept but can also be thought as leading back from the particular to the universal. This possiblity is expressed in Kant's central distinction between the determinant and the reflective judgment: "Judgment in general is the faculty of thinking the particular as contained in the universal. If the universal (the rule, principle, or law,) is given, then the judgment which subsumes the particular under it *is determinant*. . . . If, however, only the particular is given and the universal has to be found for it, then the judgment is simply *reflective*" (5:179). The simple reversal that distinguishes the reflective from the determinant is no less than a Copernican revolution in aesthetics. It makes all the difference. For, once one attempts to flesh out what is involved in the ascension from object to concept, the seeming symmetry between the two directions vanishes. In applying a given concept to a particular in the determinant judgment, we know what to look for in the object in order to determine whether it falls under the concept. But given an object, in particular an object that is singular, say a work of art, there might be many ways to speak of it and none which the object directs us to adopt. In the case of the reflective judgment we precisely do not have clear instructions to advance from the particular toward the concept. Instead of taking the truth of the judgment as our aim we are called to find meaning in and through the engagement with a singular object. To put it simply, so as to be sensitive to it, we must make sense of it.

In the determinant judgment we face the world, go out toward it, so to speak, to achieve results. Its very form, its directedness, allows the decisiveness of truth and falsity, satisfactory or unsatisfactory. We might similarly be tempted to think that the reflective aesthetic judgment on beauty ends in a decisive determination—"This is beautiful!"—but we would then merely fall prey to surface similarities and assimilate to one another very different forms. In the case of the determinant judgment the achievement of a determination is made possible by having a specific way to reach the object through the perspective of the given concept. In the case of the reflective judgment, that which gives the perspective to judgment, the concept is precisely lacking. We are not given a direction from the object toward a goal identified by a specific concept. If we now recall that interest is manifest in the concept through which we represent an object to ourselves, then the lack of a determinate direction in reflective judgment is the best manifestation of our lack of interest in the object. We have reached an initial understanding of Kant's characterization of the aesthetic judgment as disinterested.[2]

Kant's insistence on disinterestedness results both from the sensitivity to the feature of our aesthetic experience and from a reflection on the possibility of a critique of the faculty of judgment. Insofar as a judgment has an interest, we do not exhibit fully the capacity to judge. For that interest subordinates the *faculty* of judgment to the faculty of desire; it makes judgment dependent on something external to itself. We judge for the sake of something, that is, not for the sake of judging itself. Yet, in a critique of judgment we have primarily judgment in mind and ask about the faculty of judgment as it speaks for itself without it being the handmaid of other faculties. Only insofar as judgment has a field in which it wields the highest authority (while not quite being legislative) is there a justification for a philosophical critique of that faculty. There is a pure judgment if there is a disinterested judgment, that is, if we can judge merely for judging's sake. This turns out to be the possibility opened by the aesthetic judgment.

The term 'judgment,' one should note, is often used to mean the result rather than the act or activity of judging. In most cases we might readily assume that act and result form one whole, the one being inseparable from the other. And yet, just as Kant asks us to consider pure willing, willing as such, apart from its ends, the aesthetic judgment never aims to achieve anything but only to exhibit the capacity for judgment itself.[3] We might rephrase the preceding conclusion by saying that all that counts is simply to judge. Thus a contrast is formed between judging for the sake of something other than judgment (at the service of another faculty) and judging as such. There is a peculiar simplicity to the aesthetic judgment. It requires neither knowledge nor the adoption of any end. It rather considers something simply insofar as it asks to be judged.

Yet, this may seem to only complicate the picture, for how are we to assess the rightness of a judgment that has no aim apart from judging, given that objective notions of goodness and truth cannot play a role in determining its validity? The general form of an answer is clear: Even if no objective criterion of agreement with the object can be given, we still can appeal to the subjective side of agreement, namely pleasure. Subjectively speaking, agreement pleases. Asking about the validity of judgment in itself, that is, asking about the agreement of mind and thing apart from a given conceptual determination, we remain with the mere ground of pleasure. To simply judge is manifest in being pleased with the object:

> The beautiful is what *simply* pleases. (5:210)

> *All one wants to know* is whether the *mere* representation of the object is to my liking. (5:205)

> [The beautiful is a matter of] simple approval. (5:207)

What could be simpler than being pleased? Of course it must be the *right* pleasure. For such pleasure cannot be taken in the satisfaction of desire, dependent as it is on interest. Neither can it be an agreeable sensation that certain things effectively cause, for then the judgment would be utterly contingent. But what else can pleasure be?

Doing away with the interest, which provided impetus, direction, and goal, seems to leave us not only without a clear sense of the kind of pleasure we can have in the object but even without any reason to judge at all. Our capacity to judge needs to be engaged yet not reach a verdict. In order to equally avoid paralysis and resolution, the judgment must be an advance, be on the way, without reaching an end. One might also say that the *way* we engage the object is critical to the aesthetic judgment. The aesthetic judgment has a way with the object without knowing one is on the right track. To only advance without having a prior goal, a clear direction, might be captured by the sense that one thing leads to another. In such a state one feels an increase or intensification that points to an inner rational, which we cannot fathom. We sense that there is *something to it* without quite being able to say exactly what it is. But what is the field of advance, assuming it is not literally space? What is the measure of proximity or intimacy with the object? And how do we remain true to it? Can one feel oriented without any signposts determining a direction in which to go?

This may sound more mysterious than it actually is: Don't we know, for instance, of the intimacy created by a lively conversation? Neither side orchestrates the encounter for its own interests; neither is self-effacing, and precisely then it goes on, of itself unplanned and uncoerced. The conversation may even bring out those involved, not quite as they are used to thinking of themselves but rather insofar as they have potential for freely pursuing the exchange. It is indeed utterly pleasing in that it goes on. Plea-sure is taken in the free yet harmonious advance in a space of meaning. Is significance similarly that in which aesthetic judgment finds its measure?

What is significant engages me, it is such as to reveal me to myself. This does not mean imposing my subjective outlook on what is to be judged. Intimacy with the beautiful must be revealing, must bring me out not quite as I know myself but, so to speak, in my potentiality as a judging subject. The aesthetic judgment is grounded on "a feeling which the sub-ject has of itself and of the manner in which it is affected by the represen-tation" (5:204). It is not the case that, in general, when I feel something, I can feel myself in that feeling. If I feel pain in my leg, it would be at best strange to say that I have a feeling of myself in that pain. If I am in pain, then *it* concentrates my attention. What is then the condition in which a feeling can be said to reveal me to myself? Note that Kant takes pleasure and displeasure to be measures of the subject's "feeling of life." As opposed to taking pleasure to be a specific, qualitatively determined sensation, speaking of it in terms of a feeling of life suggests a certain energetic move-ment, liveliness, whose source would not necessarily be the body's state but can also be our mental activity. The animation of the mind is that wherein the subject senses itself. In the reflective judgment it is as though my mind as a whole is engaged by the representation.[4]

The judgment gives me the feeling of my capacity to judge rather than being merely a determinate actualization of that capacity. Kant's words suggest that to judge aesthetically without expecting any benefit to knowl-edge would make present the entire faculty of representation:

> Here the representation is referred wholly to the subject, and what is more to his feeling of life—under the name of pleasure and displeasure—and this forms the basis of a quite separate faculty of discriminating and estimating, that contributes nothing to knowl-edge. *All it does is to compare the given representation in the subject with the entire faculty of representations of which the mind is conscious in the feeling of its state.* (5:204, my emphasis)

The reflective judgment returns me to myself. But it is not an immediate reflexive relation of the subject to itself that closes it off from the world.

Rather, the subject is reflected by the lively engagement with the object. It is by being reflected by what is beautiful that I am returned to myself, differently, sensing my capacity as a judging subject. It is the very sense, the feeling, that a faculty, a power, is revealed in judging that becomes the measure, the internal standard for the rightness of the judgment.

At this point I would like to shift slightly the angle of investigation of the first moment and consider what is added by Kant's emphasis that the judgment must not rely on an interest in *the real existence* of the object. Understanding what is added by this idea of real existence will allow us to grasp more clearly the sense in which Kant does not concern himself in this moment with anything belonging to our psychological makeup but makes a logical point concerning the very form of the aesthetic judgment. That point might be obscured by relying too much on Kant's somewhat simplistic examples of the presence of interest, for instance, that of the "Iroquois *sachem* who said that nothing in Paris pleased him better than the eating-houses" (5:204). But desire and interest certainly have subtler ways of manifesting themselves than when I crave to eat something.

To clarify, think of Kant's emphasis on "real existence" in relation to our perceptual awareness of beauty. The reality of the object, its effective presence, is precisely manifest in sensation. Sensation is "the real in perception" (5:148). In stressing the disinterest in the real existence of the object, Kant does not preclude perceiving, for surely an aesthetic judgment requires the experience of its object. We do not judge in the abstract or in theory. The point is then that what is real in perception cannot be the ground of judgment. The real, or the given of sensation cannot be judged to be beautiful:

> A mere color, e.g. the green of a lawn, a mere tone . . . say that of a violin, is declared by most people to be beautiful in itself although both have as their ground merely the matter of representation, namely mere sensation and on that account deserve to be called only agreeable. (5:224)

The following claim makes clear what it is for judgment to become independent of real existence, of sensation: "It is quite plain that in order to say that the object is *beautiful,* and to show that I have taste, everything turns on what I make of this representation in myself [*was ich aus dieser Vorstellung in mir selbst mache*], and not on any factor which makes me dependent on the real existence of the object" (5:205, translation modified). It is by making something of what is given that I free myself from the dependence of interest, from the actuality of the real. Making oneself independent from interest cannot just be relinquishing it. One cannot decide to be disinterested without further ado. Disinterest is not, in other words, a preparatory necessary condition for judging adequately. It is not as though in entering a museum I check my coat and bag and switch off my cell phone as well as my interests. It is what I do in judging that allows the state of disinterest. Nothing short of my involvement with the beautiful itself can detach me from interest. Beauty has the power to detach us from the demands of real existence.

The aesthetic judgment takes place in a space of reflection that precludes being merely affected by the object's actual existence. Indeed, Kant speaks not of perceiving beauty but of *contemplating* it: "The judgment of taste is simply contemplative" (5:209). And contemplation, like reflection, is not without thoughtfulness. Beauty, one might say, makes us reflective. There is a sense of delay in reflection, of taking one's time rather than being decisive, of a contemplative rather than a committed state. But such absorption does not mean indulging in sweet reveries, for it is at the same time dwelling upon that which is beautiful, a devotion to the singular thing with which one is faced.

One could also say that an actual property can come into my judgment only insofar as I can make something of it as it comes to *play a part* in my reflection. We of course identify a painting, say, as a material object having certain properties. But our aesthetic experience does not take the form of identifying such and such characteristics in the object, whose presence would then justify calling it beautiful (even though it is as if we locate beauty wholly in the object). Beauty exists only in the space opened by the subject in being responsive to the object, and such space of possibilities of advance must be distinguished from any collection of actual objective properties of an existing object. As Kant suggests, a certain playfulness of the imagination and the understanding is involved in its opening. Through these considerations what comes into question is precisely the reality of the experience of the beautiful. Being unconcerned with the real existence of the *object* might mean precisely that the beautiful is not quite an *object* of experience. Whether this dissociation from the real leaves room to attribute another kind of veracity to aesthetic experience is a question it would be premature to develop here in any detail.

§2. The Second Moment

From the last considerations it becomes clearer why the first moment, centered on disinterestedness, leads to the consideration of the communicability of the aesthetic judgment, that is, to the fuller articulation of the role of meaning in aesthetic judgment. The second moment of the 'Analytic of the Beautiful' is summed up by the characterization "The *beautiful* is that which, apart from a concept, pleases universally." But, following the account of the first moment, we should insist from the start that this characterization need not be interpreted to mean that no concepts are involved in the activity of judging, only that such concepts should not bring reflection to an end by determining the thing of beauty by way of a specific, definite concept.

The second moment contains some of the most striking elements of Kant's analysis. To understand it properly one needs both to underscore the singularity of the aesthetic judgment and, despite or because of that singularity, its peculiar mode of universality. Insofar as the field of aesthetics is subject to a transcendental investigation it must have a universal character. But Kant starts by noting the obvious fact that the dimension of universality in aesthetic judgment cannot be understood in terms of the range of things deemed beautiful. Since a generalization essentially involves a determinant use of concepts, it cannot provide the form of universality of aesthetic judgments. There is no aesthetic judgment of the form "all roses are beautiful" as there might be a cognitive judgment to the effect that all roses are red.[5] Not that aesthetic generalizations turn out to be incorrect, but rather the aesthetic judgment can be said to be *essentially* singular. So, before even addressing the nature of the universality in that field, something must be said about this peculiar aesthetic singularity. Indeed, the singularity of the aesthetic judgment cannot be explained in terms of the application of concepts; thus it cannot be modeled upon the *logically* singular judgment. Attempting instead to characterize singularity by reference to the register of intuition would be equally problematic, for it would make the judgment too dependent on actual existence in space and time and thus on causal efficacy, which is always the source of agreeableness rather than reflective pleasure. But how could we account for singularity other than, say, by a definite description or by reference to actual spatiotemporal presence?

In passing judgment, it is essential to be in the presence of the thing in its singularity. An aesthetic judgment cannot be arrived at in theory. But that presence cannot be that of the actual existent which could only be the cause of agreeable sensation. To be in touch with what is judged, to have it present to mind is essentially distinguished from it *causing* us pleasure. As I argued earlier, to avoid the merely sensuous is to make something of the representation in me. But it is not as though I merely add to the actual properties of the object a further external and arbitrarily chosen meaning. Rather, to make something of an aspect of the object is first and foremost to assume that its identity 'in beauty' cannot be dissociated from the whole of which it partakes. It is this meaningful presence of the whole in my involvement with its parts which can be properly called singular, or essentially one. This would mean that no aspect has any independent determination apart from the connectedness of the whole, conversely that totality is presupposed in attending to the significance of any part. So as to distinguish this unity of significance, which is evoked by the beautiful thing, from the unity that is a matter of conceptual determination, we could say that the unity in the experience of the beautiful is not a result of the synthesis of concepts but rather resembles the totalization in an idea. Since one can only *strive* toward the realization of the unity of the idea in experience, we can say, following our discussion of the first moment, that beauty is singular precisely by the way it keeps reflection constantly in play. To be committed to the singularity of the beautiful is to insist that no specific determination can in itself be final or definitive, that is, bring reflection to an end.

Bearing this understanding of singularity in mind, we can now inquire after the dimension of universality characteristic of the aesthetic judgment. Such universality cannot be referred to an objective law, whether in the constitution of the object (as in cognition) or in what ought to determine subjects (as in morality). Kant distinguishes between the universality one can attribute to the subject matter of judgment and the subjective universality which judgments can have, that is, the universal agreement all subjects should converge upon in judging that subject matter. But the question is precisely how such subjective universality is to be possible without an objective subject matter to agree upon. Moreover, the very attempt to think in terms of agreement with others feels external to what really matters in judging. Just as the object of beauty appears always singular, so *my* response is what I should rely upon. It is not pleasure in general but *my* pleasure that matters. And, the object speaks to me, as it were returns my gaze, only when I trust myself in judging it. I do not ask myself first how others would judge, and only then make up my mind. Nor would it be right to say that I judge for myself and then infer from a reflection on the condition in which I find myself that all would have judged similarly in these conditions. Rather, to retain this self-reliance, universality is internalized into the very making of the judgment. In passing judgment I speak for others; in giving meaning to what is singular, I take myself to be representative. The aesthetic judgment is pronounced with a universal voice as the judge of taste ". . . judges not merely for himself, but for all men, and then speaks of beauty as if it were a property of things" (5:212).

The domain of the political provides a ready analogy to clarify the holding together of individuality and universality in being representative, in speaking with a universal voice. The representative must express himself, or give voice to what he stands for. In so doing he is not merely an emissary of those who elected him. He must speak for all rather than advance narrow sectarian interests. In other words, he speaks for the common good (or the general will), albeit from a stance determined by his convictions and principles. Even if he is guided by explicit, agreed-upon principles, there is much to articulate which may have been left implicit, and, more importantly, he must exemplify what it is for such principles to *apply* to the actual shifting circumstances.[6]

The aesthetic judgment is essentially representative because what one testifies to has yet to be articulated. There are no generally agreed-upon rules or properties whose presence would make the object beautiful. The judge of taste "speaks of beauty *as if* it were a property of things." (5:212). To pronounce a judgment on what is essentially singular is thus not to speak of what we in fact agree upon, but to speak for an *idea* of universal

agreement. "[The] universal voice is . . . only an idea" (5:216). Whereas
certain objects are examples of concepts or instances of *general* laws, the
universality pertaining to the unity of the idea can only be expressed by
the representativeness of subjects. The subject must be manifest in his
judgment, meaning that the way of judging, must show the judgment to be
representative of an idea of agreement. Merely to claim that one is judging
with the idea in mind carries no authority. It is only by making the judgment itself involve advance toward the idea, so to speak show in judging
the way the idea can never be fully and determinately realized in experience, that one can be representative of it. Such tendency in the movement
of the mind is what I believe Kant means to express in the notion of "purposiveness without purpose," which is central to the third moment of the
'Analytic of the Beautiful.'

It is now possible to better understand, at least in the case of the beauty
of art, how our conceptual capacity can be involved in judgment apart
from a determinate concept. Indeed, there is no difficulty in finding some
concept or other to apply to beautiful works. The problem is that a certain
use of concepts will stifle judging by eventuating in a judgment, imposing
a preconception, as though judging beauty is determining the properties
of an object. Thus what is demanded is to be attuned to the potential in
the singularity of beauty, to its being pregnant with significance. In the
reflective judgment concepts not only evolve from the singular but also
strive to remain true to it, to do justice to its beauty. It is in having reflection avoid an end point, that is, in being devoted to the singularity of
beauty, that the judgment of taste speaks for an idea of universal agreement. Taking beauty to be a singular whole precisely allows the deployment of our imagination and our conceptual capacity to be guided solely
by an idea of universal agreement.

What is exemplified by the judgment is thus nothing more than the
possibility of an advance of reflection in relation to that singularity which
is beautiful: ". . . nothing is postulated in the judgment of taste but such a
universal voice in respect of delight that is not mediated by concepts; consequently, only the *possibility* of an aesthetic judgment capable of being at
the same time deemed valid for every one" (5:216). To speak of "the possibility of an aesthetic judgment" is not to say that the judgment is only
possibly correct, but rather that it inherently involves showing a possibility

of relating one's experience to the idea of agreement. To thus show agreement to be possible does not preclude other ways of relating to the idea in being involved with the object, but rather calls for them. Indeed, it is the very gap between the idea and any attempt to give it presence (which, of necessity, will be lacking) that requires further exemplifications. Far from damaging the universality of the aesthetic judgment, the multiplicity of takes on, say, a work of art, is precisely adequate to its nature. It is not incompatible with the idea of the universal voice but precisely expresses it. In a community of taste, agreement need not be thought of in terms of identical responses to beauty. Rather, there is agreement in being equally attuned to the singularity of beauty and thus attuned to one another by way of the beautiful. Just as in the realm of ends I view myself equally as legislator and subject, in the community of taste I am a party to a conversation that gives expression to beauty.

The possibility of a plurality of responses to a work of art does not imply any relativism of the form "To each his own taste." What is encompassed are other possibilities of finding the work meaningful, that is, other possibilities of making something of the object in reflection. Moreover, an aesthetic judgment involves a demand on others. In a cognitive judgment, I may expect you to agree with me, but there would be no point making a demand. If you do not see the table to be white as I do, I may suggest you check your eyesight, but my perceptual judgment would not involve a demand from you. It would be similarly problematic to demand others to act morally, not because they ought not to do so. Rather, as a moral agent I place a demand on myself, and by demanding from others I risk moralizing. Furthermore, to conceive of a demand being internal to the judgment of taste would not imply that after I make the judgment, and am, so to speak, convinced of its validity for myself, I then go and demand or require others to agree. (Just as in speaking with a universal voice, speaking for others, I need not first ask for their permission.) One can produce a demand precisely by judging for oneself, by exhibiting what it is to be so absorbed by beauty. A demand can arise, say, by expressing oneself in ways that are *demanding*. The language of the judgment produces a demand when it is higher or when it shows how one can be resting on one's own ground to freely open meaning in the object. In so judging one may be attracting or shaming others but either way placing a demand upon them. In passing an aesthetic judgment "we are suitors for the agreement of every one else" (5:237). The language of the suitor is tempting, but he also must be ready "often enough to put up with rude dismissal" (5:214), for he cannot defend himself with an argument.

Actual communication is not assumed to be internal to the aesthetic judgment but rather communicability. Since my pleasure is taken in making something of my experience, I have an active share in it, and it is that which allows of communication. This is not pleasure in *communicating* in fact and being understood by others. Indeed, that latter pleasure is threatened by an interest in society and cannot be the ground of the aesthetic judgment. The pleasure must be in the free opening of reflection itself thus in *communicability* rather than in the satisfaction of our interest in actual communication. Reflection allows beauty to be in common.

Just as the universal voice is not reducible to a common reaction to an object of delight in ideal conditions, communicability is not to be confused with having different subjects be in the same state or condition. It is not a residual state of mind, which would be found equally in all those who free themselves of any interest in the face of the object of judgment. The judgment is not merely a pleasurable reaction to the object, which, upon reflection and recognition that no interest is involved, is then expected to arise in anyone with the same faculties under the same conditions. This would make the pleasure antecedent to communicability, and indistinguishable from a pleasure of the senses. Rather, as Kant puts it in section 9, which he calls "the key to the critique of taste," "it is the universal capacity for being communicated incident to the mental state in the given representation which, as the subjective condition of the judgment of taste, must be fundamental, with the pleasure in the object as its consequent" (5:217).

Yet, how can communicability precede pleasure? What is it that is communicated if not the pleasure taken in the object? To be sure, communicability does not precede pleasure temporally speaking but constitutes its condition. My pleasure is in the reflective engagement with the object. A condition is pleasurable, by definition, when it tends to further itself. Pleasure is not the consciousness of a specific *quality* but rather "the consciousness of the causality of a representation in respect of the state of the Subject as one tending to *preserve a continuance* of that state may here be said to denote in a general way what is called pleasure" (5:220). The enhanced activity of the mind, the furthering that shows the mind's potential, in giving meaningful expression to beauty *is* the pleasure of the aesthetic judgment: "The consciousness of mere formal finality in the play of the cognitive faculties of the Subject attending a representation whereby an object is given *is* the pleasure itself" (5:222, my emphasis).

An objection might arise from the identification of the pleasure with the very activity of our faculties in judging. Indeed, in that case, how can there be a mistaken aesthetic judgment? Such a mistaken judgment is assumed possible by Kant in his discussion of the second moment:

> For himself he can be certain on the point from his mere consciousness of the separation of everything belonging to the agreeable and the good from the delight remaining to him; and this is all for which he promises himself the agreement of every one—a claim which, under these conditions, he would also be warranted in making, were it not that he frequently sinned against them, and thus passed an erroneous judgment of taste. (5:216)

Thus it appears that, similarly to the moral case and the inscrutability of the grounds of the will, we may have in the case of the aesthetic a possibility of self-deception regarding the validity of one's judgment. But does that mean that before passing an aesthetic judgment one should engage in soul searching to determine whether there are no hidden interests one would have at that moment? If the furthering of the mind has the kind of explicit manifestation I argue it has, then it would be what provides us the *best criterion* for being disinterested. One could even say that conscious reflection about what interests I may or may not have would not yield more certainty and has a better chance of being itself deluded than the feeling we have in the enlargement of our mind, to which we have to be faithful in the aesthetic judgment. Disinterestedness is manifest in the free play of our faculties. The latter is the best sign that I have no underlying motivation.

Yet, another more complex possibility of a mistaken judgment can be conceived if we take into account the dimension of agreement in judgment that is presupposed in speaking in a universal voice. For it is possible that one does not receive the concurrence of others even in the long run.

The situation here is similar to what Rousseau tells us about the general will. Even if one has deliberated from the proper point of view, it might still be the case that the general will is different, and one is then, in Rousseau's famous phrase, forced to be free. Similarly, one might say that we learn in the sphere of the aesthetic both how the individual can speak for the common and how the constitution of community can teach the individual to recognize that what he takes as inmost conviction is *merely* private to him (hopefully this is something he will remember as youthful enthusiasm rather than bitter disillusionment).

The question of the possibility of a mistaken aesthetic judgment opens the broader issue of the place of negation or the negative in aesthetics. Is it the case that, just as we described a state of mind that we could call pleasurable in our response to beauty, there would be specific displeasure that would yield a negative aesthetic judgment? Consider the case of explaining to someone why a certain painting, though manifestly the result of talent, still fails to be a significant work of art. We might have much to say about why the failed work of art fails. It might even be easier than articulating our response to the beautiful work. Nevertheless, we need not assume that our negative judgment constitutes a state of mind in which there is that movement of our faculties found in judging beauty. It is as though we can say all too well what is wrong with a bad work of art. Bad works fall short *in known ways.* There is nothing surprising in the way in which a work is bad, whereas there is always an element of wonder in the opening to beauty.

This case is different from what we would call a judgment of ugliness. Ugliness seems to be the contrasting notion to beauty, just as cold is to warm. Of course, not all that is not beautiful is ugly. Most things appear neither beautiful nor ugly, at least in our everyday interaction with them. In the face of ugliness we would recoil from the object. This itself precludes the movement of the mind characteristic of the aesthetic judgment. Indeed, if it is the strengthening or quickening of the movement of the mind that constitutes the reflective judgment, it would seem that the dissociation of the mind from the object in displeasure would not yield a negative aesthetic judgment, but rather would take us out of the sphere of reflective judgment altogether. It is significant therefore that Kant takes fine art to be able to neutralize ugliness: "Where fine art gives evidence of its superiority is in the beautiful description it gives of things that in nature would be ugly or displeasing. The Furies, diseases, devastations of war, and the like can (as evils) be very beautifully described, nay even represented in pictures" (5:312). I take it that this is further evidence for the claim I advanced, that all that matters in beauty is what I make of the representation, not anything given as such.[7]

I leave for the second part of this study the discussion of the central case of the presence of the negative in aesthetics, namely the feeling of the sublime.

§3. The Third Moment

The third moment introduces one of the most important elements of Kant's analysis: the notion of form. As he puts it in the title of section 11, "The sole foundation of the judgment of taste is the FORM OF FINAL-ITY of an object (or mode of representing it)" (5:221). This formal character of Kant's aesthetics can give rise to many misinterpretations. In trying to properly understand Kant's notion of form let us rephrase the underlying intuition of the definition of the reflective judgment. In a determinant judgment we merely ask whether an object falls under a given concept. With the reflective judgment, our sensitivity to the singular thing facing us is manifest in the *affinity* between the concepts we find and the object facing us. The conceptual space grows out of the singular thing, remaining true not of it but to it. The very adequacy of the reflective judgment would depend on finding the relevant terms for the given thing rather than imposing a concept on it, one based on our general knowledge (thus ultimately depending on a prior determinant judgment). Or to put it more strongly, we don't want merely to say something right; we feel the demand to account for that singularity *just right* in words, as though the concepts deployed strive to come together as a proper name.

But how are we to understand that notion of relevance? And how are we to explain what it is for concepts to come together or gather around a singularity? In relation to the first and second moments, the rightness in the use of concepts was identified in the way they lead on, that is, insofar as they open to further reflection. In making a reflective judgment we find concepts that further our experience with the object. In contrast, the determinant judgment involves saying something definite that halts the advance of reflection. It is the assertion that characterizes the determinant judgment. The truth in the sense we often have that beauty escapes language might be captured by the way nothing is asserted or said in the aesthetic judgment. And yet it is not because the experience of beauty is mute, but rather because something is *shown by* the ways our mind comes together in relating to the beautiful thing. We do not say anything definite about beauty but allow it to grow on us by deploying reflection that is true to its singularity.

Kant speaks of the aesthetic judgment as providing a presentation (*Darstellung*), distinguishing it from the representation (*Vorstellung*) of the object in the determinant judgment (see, for example, 5:192, 5:351–352). What is presented is laid before us, open to view. By representing something in a judgment, on the other hand, we bring the object under a concept, grasp it from a standpoint. The aesthetic judgment is to be understood over and above the assertion (which is always a determinate state of affairs), insofar as it presents or opens a *space of meaning* in the reflection on the object.

To take the idea of *opening* such a space as fundamental to the aesthetic judgment implies that we do not try to understand beauty, at least insofar as that means grasping a certain content communicated. Opening is also to be distinguished from openness, at least when the latter is understood on the model of mere sensuous receptivity. It is not an unfocused state of waiting for something to affect us, or an indeterminate condition in which one's utmost concern would be *not* to have interests.[8] Our engagement with the object must bring the mind into an energetic movement to produce that opening, to have that breadth of reflection. The opening of such a space is the presentation of form.[9] Form, then, is not only identified in the object as the origin of the movement of the mind but is also, at the same time, that which is made present by that movement.

The notion of form has been used in a variety of ways in the philosophical tradition as well as in Kant's writings. In the *Critique of Pure Reason* Kant conceives of space and time to be the forms of our intuition and takes the categories to be the forms of our thinking about objects of experience. In considering the specific use Kant makes of the notion of form in the *Critique of Judgment*, it must, from the start, be contrasted with a common use of that notion in aesthetics which associates it with an order, configuration or structure arrived at when we abstract from representational contents.

The distinction between form and such structural matters can be clarified by aligning it with the distinction between possibility and actuality. Whereas a structure or configuration is just the representation of a specific determinate fact (albeit one that seemingly does not contain recognizable representations), to present a form would be to have the representation appear against the background of its conditions of possibility. The advance of reflection is what makes for the ever more articulate presence of those conditions in our experience of the singular object of beauty. Thus, the distinction between what can be said or represented in a determinant judgment and what must be shown or presented in the aesthetic judgment is another way of formulating the independence of the latter from actual properties of the object. The presentation of form always shows more than what is actually given to the senses in perception.

Kant's characterization of the movement that opens the space of form involves what is probably the single most famous expression of the *Critique of Judgment*, namely the harmonious *free play* of the faculties. The notion of play has already been invoked by Kant in his 'First Critique.' It serves him there to distinguish that movement of the imagination which is a mere subjective play of representations and to contrast it, unfavorably, with the function of the imagination in objective knowledge, as it is bringing together intuitive representation guided by a concept. In the 'Third Critique,' Kant gives a role to play itself. Moreover, he speaks of the free play not only of the imagination but rather of *both* faculties: the imagination and the understanding. In the aesthetic one is happily, or at least pleasurably, abandoning any claims to objectivity, though not thereby giving up on any use of the understanding, which remains a key player in the possibility of an aesthetic judgment.

So as to clarify the dimensions of the idea of free play, let me start by suggesting a certain analogy whose limits I will point to after elaborating it. Consider what we would call a good (even sometimes a beautiful) game of basketball. It might be, for instance, a game where the teams are a match for each other. Neither is too obviously better than the other; neither too obviously sets the tone or pace of the game. It would be as if each team brings the other to excel, as though the play is intensified by their balance of power. It is further a game in which we would have the manifestations of all sides of basketball, offense and defense, individual virtuosity and team play, or, to put it simply, it would be a game that shows us the possibilities of basketball as such. This is not just a matter of playing by the rules: Of course, there are rules of basketball, but both a good and a bad game of basketball are played according to the rules. It would be a game that stands for what basketball can be.

The difficulty with transposing this analogy to the field of play of aesthetic judgment is clear. It involves the notion of the perfection of a certain kind of end-oriented activity. Yet, Kant stresses that the movement of the mind constituting the aesthetic judgment has no purpose. It involves purposiveness without purpose. Recognizing this difficulty might lead to two different readings of Kant's claim that the aesthetic judgment involves purposiveness without purpose. According to the first, which I called earlier the minimalist option, the absence of a concept of an end means that the aesthetic play of the faculties is to be taken to be wholly devoid of *any* concepts. But it would then be hard to see how Kant thinks that the understanding could at all be involved in such a play (for what is it for the faculty of concepts to be active without concepts?). Alternatively, we could clarify what it is to think of concepts coming together in such a way that no determinate end or overarching conceptual determination would be in sight. Put more precisely, even though concepts may have exact boundaries with regard to the objects falling under them, they nevertheless might be open with regard to the way they come together systematically. It is in relation to this coming together of concepts purposively, yet without an overarching determination of the end, that one would open enough space for play that involves both imagination *and* understanding.

A game played often involves both a structuring of space and time as well as what we would call moves of the game. In the most common cases, the spatial dimension is determined by the boundaries of a board or field, and the temporal dimension by the division of temporal segments of a game. What is readily understood in the case of a game needs to be translated into formal characteristics of the movement of the mind in the aesthetic judgment. This movement appears at first to involve contrary characterizations. Kant speaks on the one hand of the restfulness in our contemplation of the beautiful; that is, he conceives of repose as essential to that state. On the other hand Kant thinks of it as a state that "strengthens and reproduces itself" as a "quickening of the faculties." That tension between movement and rest is further echoed by the characterization of the pleasure involved in the judgment of taste. Kant's definition of pleasure as "the consciousness of the causality of a representation in respect to the state of the Subject as one tending to preserve a continuance of that state" (5: 220) emphasizes the aspect of rest or inertial motion. But it is the developing movement that is required to distinguish such pleasure both from the state of agreeableness caused by pleasing objects and from the satisfaction provided by attaining an end. The same tension is also apparent in Kant's explication of "dwelling" upon beauty, which, while denoting a restful condition, is compatible with activity and is opposed to "lingering," which is merely passive: "We *dwell* on the contemplation of the beautiful because this contemplation strengthens and reproduces itself. The case is analogous (but analogous only) to the way we linger on a charm in the representation of an object which keeps arresting the attention, the mind all the while remaining passive" (5:222). In spatial terms, dwelling, one might say, involves one's presence in an expanse, and is manifest in the movement that explores, or opens, it for us. Lingering, in contrast, leaves us fixed in a spot, in passive attachment to an object, or a specific state of affairs.

We might suggest a way to resolve the tension by recalling the claim I presented in the discussion of the first moment, that what is at stake in the aesthetic judgment is the presentation of a capacity of the mind. We testify to a potential, that is, to our capacity, by opening possibilities of meaning of the thing presented. Viewed from the perspective of the subject, then, in a certain sense the state of mind is always the same, for it must constantly testify to the faculty of representation as a whole. But since the presentation of that capacity of the mind differs from a specific use of it, it is only the strengthening of that movement that testifies to a *potential*.

Let us try to put the point in terms of a figure that might have been on Kant's mind. Potential is manifested not in inertial but rather in accelerated movement. It is precisely the potential of our faculties that needs to be shown, and thus the movement is a *quickening* of those faculties. Indeed, following that figure one might say that acceleration is essential to avoid a determinate relation between the faculties. A determinate relation, a specific use of our faculties, would be a particular ratio, a particular speed of our faculties, so to speak ($v = d/t$). The quickening is a constant change of ratio, yet one with an essential progression to it ($a = d/t^2$). As

Kant puts it in the fourth moment, ". . . this disposition of the cognitive powers has a relative proportion differing with the diversity of the objects that are given. However, there must be one in which this internal relation suitable for quickening (one faculty by the other) is best adapted for both mental powers in respect to cognition generally" (5:238).

To speak of what is best adapted for cognition generally might suggest an average or a common factor present in all states of cognition. We might be tempted further to take Kant's claim that in the judgment upon beauty the faculties are brought together to an *indefinite* activity to mean that such a state of mind is a vague conglomerate of perception and pleasure, something less than conscious and surely not definite enough to put into words. And we might even assume that, because it is a state that occurs wherever we are confronted by beauty, it must be something very minimal indeed, which is common to our experience of a flower and the *Mona Lisa*. Yet, the mistake might be in having too narrow or reified a notion of what a state of mind is. For Kant does not characterize a common *static* state but a form of activity, a way to reflect on or contemplate the beautiful. Such a state of mind is not confused, but rather its characterization as indefinite precisely points to the fact that no single conceptual determination can do the work. The power of the mind is precisely made evident by not "being limited to a definite cognition" (5:222). It is a state of mind identified by the inner logic of its changes, a continuous activity whose whole scope defines what it is to judge something to be beautiful. That activity can be fine tuned and exacting, while not eventuating in a conceptual determination. Similarly, by referring the judgment to "cognition generally" Kant means that what is revealed in that state is the faculty of representation as a whole. The activity of judging puts the mind in lively movement, which brings out the potential of our faculties. And that movement is nothing else than the unfolding of our meaningful experience of the object.

But what does the figure of a ratio between the imagination and the understanding really amount to? How can one speak, as Kant does in the fourth moment, of a ratio of faculties of the mind? And how does it relate to the idea of harmony that Kant attributes to the free play of the faculties? The full significance of these matters will become evident in the discussion of the fourth moment, but one might try the following provisional clarification of the language of proportion: A given concept can be broken down into characteristic component terms. For example, being a table might involve having a flat top positioned on legs and large enough for human activities such as eating and writing to take place on it. Of course, each such characterization would leave open various possibilities for what would count as a table. It would be inadvisable to try and provide a complete definition that would sharply determine the boundaries of the concept against all eventualities. There would be no point in trying to seal off every case by listing sub-concepts of the concept of being a table. We wouldn't, for instance, and not only from fear of going against fashion, introduce into the definition that a table has four legs. Put differently, we would leave some space for the imagination to apply the concept to appearances. But we would ask the imagination, which is to provide the schema of such a concept, to show some restraint, not to lose proportion. So, for instance, even if most table tops are horizontal, the imagination might give room to apply the concept to a tilted top (as in a drafting table). We can also imagine a very small and very low table for toddlers, but a top perched on thin legs two meters above the floor would not merit being called a table even if one could reach on tiptoes the food laid on it. The latter would involve a disproportionate use of the imagination relative to the given concept. Each concept, according to this figure of ratio, would have an imaginative space proportionate to it, a schematic rendering of what would count as a possible application of the concept. But we might now consider further that the spaces of different concepts are delimited by each other (so certain things might count as sitting at a table so long as table manners are not at issue). More important, for the discussion of beauty, in some cases an object might provide an occasion for bringing together, or concentrating, schematic spaces belonging to disparate concepts and creating a harmonious whole whose proportion or measure cannot be determined by the ratio of imagination and understanding of any prior concept. The sense of that overall non-calculable balance is, as I understand it, what Kant points to in his idea of harmony between the faculties in beauty.

Given this initial elaboration of the character of the harmonious relation between imagination and understanding we can turn to consider Kant's distinction between free and dependent beauty. Kant writes that "in the estimate of a free beauty (according to mere form) we have the pure judgment of taste" (5:129). This emphasis on the *purity* of the judgment of taste on free beauty might lead to a misinterpretation of the distinction between the free and the dependent, according to which only one side authentically belongs to the aesthetic. Dependent beauty would be tainted by the presence of concepts. If so, we would then expect it to be a lesser kind of beauty. Yet, it might be sufficient to point out that the ideal of beauty is the maximum of *dependent* beauty. And how could an ideal be a lesser beauty? It is rather as if purity and ideality come apart and the field of the aesthetic judgment is spanned between both. (I leave for Part IV of the book the interpretation of Kant's account of the ideal of beauty as well as the extreme manifestation of the duality of free and dependent beauty.)

I prefer therefore to read the division between the free and the dependent to be internal to beauty, so that it is the aesthetic *itself* that does not have a unitary character (understandably, one might add, given its mediating role). It is not as if that which is properly beautiful in dependent beauties is their free aspect, which emerges only when we completely ignore what they are. In judging dependent beauty, Kant emphasizes that the involvement of a concept of the object does not collapse the aesthetic judgment upon a determinant judgment of perfection: "Strictly speaking, perfection neither gains by beauty, nor beauty by perfection," but rather "there results a gain to the *entire faculty* of our representative power when harmony prevails between both states of mind" (5:231). Both Kant's reference to a gain to the *entire faculty of representation*, as well as the assessment of the movement of the mind in terms of harmony (rather than a specific ratio of the two sides), proves that we have in dependent beauty just as important a manifestation of the aesthetic field as would be found in free beauties.

As is clear from Kant's examples of dependent beauty, we delimit in certain ways the expanse of reflection opened by the imagination and the understanding. "Much might be added to a building that would immediately please the eye," Kant writes, "were it not intended for a church. A figure might be beautified with all manner of flourishes and light but regular lines, as is done by the New Zealanders with their tattooing, were we dealing with anything but the figure of a human being" (5:230). But this proportional employment of the imagination, brought about by taking into account what the object is, not only leaves room for freedom, but makes it all the more significant. This is obvious in art, where restrictions such as

the conventions of a genre not only limit but also enable and enrich reflection. We exhibit the freedom adequate to reflection on *that* kind of
thing, to the estimation of *such* beauty. A free beauty such as a flowing
ornament might not be restricted by any concept, but the complete freedom we would have to follow it our way would be rather insignificant and
poor (limited, say, to *choosing* certain paths in two-dimensional space).
Conversely, we might be inspired to reflection by the specific proportions
of a building precisely *because* it is a church. And a thick characterization
of human action in a drama that brings into play its different dimensions
affords the *breadth and depth* for our freedom of reflection, which are not
available as one looks at a flower or a bird.

Is the space of form opened by the movement of the mind something
inherent in the thing itself, or is such form added to it by the imagination?
As always in the 'Third Critique' we could argue that it is neither or both.
Kant speaks of form just as much in relation to the movement of the mind
as in relation to the object. He writes equally of the form of finality of an
object and the formal finality in the play of the cognitive faculties.[10] Form
is opened up and presented by the movement of the mind and it is the horizon that delimits the reflection. Just as the movement of the mind reveals the faculty of representation as a whole, so the corresponding revelation of the thing as a limited or formed totality can be called the intuiting
of the conditions that make it significant as wholly present and embodied
in it. Beauty, one might say, is a field of embodied meaningfulness or experienced significance. In the aesthetic, purposive form is dissociated from
action and aim, as well as from the teleological explication of the order in
nature, and comes to be associated with the very experience of our human
world as significant, as endlessly involving in and of itself.

A last inflection of the concept of play might serve to express how the
movement of the mind and the possibilities of the object arise together.
We speak of play not only in relation to games but also in the context of
playing a role or a character in theater or more generally when, say, we
speak of children playing at being an airplane or a train. Play and mimetic
capacity are closely related. We might not readily recognize this dimension in Kant's account of the aesthetic though it is central to his understanding of form. It is encapsulated in the duality expressing the internal

relation between the finality of the form of the object and the finality of the state of mind in representing to ourselves the object. As the parentheses in the heading of section 11 in the third moment make clear we have the one with, or by way of, the other: "The judgment of taste has nothing but the *form of purposiveness* of an object (or of the way of representing it) as its ground" (5:221). We have in effect the formation of a space which is neither wholly in the mind nor wholly in the object but rather a meeting place of the mind and the object or a space in which the capacity of the mind is identified by the involvement with the object and the form of the object revealed by the movement of the mind.

In other words, it is not sufficient to point out that the beautiful engages the mind's faculties and bring them into play. It is further necessary to characterize what in the object is revealed by this play of the faculties. Otherwise that movement risks being merely a private stream of associations. But conversely, it is important not to objectify form. Actual properties of things are surely fully determined, and possibilities, insofar as they are given by objective laws (such as those of physics), are similarly completely determinate. But significant human possibilities are not given once and for all; they are rather opened by our engagement with beauty.

§4. The Fourth Moment

Exemplification plays a central role in the *Critique of Judgment*. As I noted in the Introduction, the notion of the example appeared already, without being given a systematic function, in the account of judgment in the *Critique of Pure Reason*. Lacking rules, judgment in general depends on natural talent, "so-called mother wit [whose] lack no school can make good," as well as on its, albeit poor substitutes, examples which are "the go-cart of judgment" (A133/B172).

The systematic thematization of the inner relation of exemplification and natural ground is found, I want to argue, in the fourth moment of the 'Analytic of the Beautiful': "such a necessity as is thought in an aesthetic judgment . . . can only be termed *exemplary*. In other words it is a necessity of the assent of *all* to a judgment regarded as exemplifying a universal rule incapable of formulation" (5:237). It is in the aesthetic judgment that exemplification is more than a mere pedagogical aid for the awakening of a natural ability.[11] It becomes a characteristic of the necessity involved in the aesthetic judgment. It is the specific modality of the aesthetic judgment.

A connection is then formed between the second moment and the fourth moment (which further makes clear how much the four moments of Kant's account are indeed internally related parts of a unified grammar of judgment). The second moment underscored the representativeness of the judge of taste. One is representative in showing the possibility of further meaningful reflection in the subject matter. What we make of the object in reflection must in turn not appear to be artificially added; rather, it must feel as though it expressed something in the object known all along. It must feel natural or seem to be the expression of something we can call the natural ground of our common existence. If the universal voice is the to-be-formed idea of agreement, then such agreement must appear as the expression of the already given natural ground we share, as the expression of our common sense. (Indeed, one should note that the term 'mother wit,' which Kant uses in characterizing the talent for exercising the capacity for judgment in the *Critique of Pure Reason*, can also mean common sense).

Exemplification relates itself not only to the universal agreement of judging subjects, or to the idea of the universal voice but also presupposes a common natural ground. Common sense is a *presupposition* on the basis of which the universal voice is *imputed*. One can represent ideal agreement with others only by relying on one's sense of the common ground. "We are suitors for agreement from every one else, *because we are fortified with a ground common to all*" (5:237, my emphasis). The idea of universal agreement discussed in the second moment and the idea of a common sense discussed in the fourth are linked together by the logic of exemplification: Universal agreement (the artificial) is formed by taking oneself to express the given ground in common (the natural). We can speak for all only by resting on, sensing, that unexpressed ground in common. Voice puts its trust in sense, and sense needs to be given voice.

In common sense our sensible awareness of the beautiful is internally related to our possible attunement to others. That latter aspect, of common sense as a social or public sense, is most evident as Kant returns to the term in section 40, long after completing the elaboration of the grammar of the four moments in the 'Analytic of the Beautiful.' I will start my analysis from this later account and gradually lead back from it to the understanding of the common sense presented in the fourth moment. ". . . [By] the name *sensus communis*," Kant writes, "is to be understood the idea of a *public sense*, i.e. a critical faculty which in its reflective act takes account *(a priori)* of the mode of representation of every one else, in order, *as it were*, to weigh its judgment with the collective reason of mankind" (5:293). This idea of a common sense is to be distinguished from a prevalent use of the term to denote "a minimum expected from anyone who lays claim to the name of a human being." That minimum is what is intended by the identification of "common" with "vulgar." As Kant points out, "to possess [that which is encountered everywhere] is certainly not an advantage or an honor" (ibid.). It surely cannot be the ground of the capacity to judge aesthetically. Nor should we confuse aesthetic common sense with common human understanding or what Kant also calls sound understanding. The latter is guided by three fundamental maxims: "(1) to think for oneself; (2) to think from the standpoint of every one else; (3) always to think consistently" (5:294). These are formal characterizations of the use of the understanding: The first avoids passivity, that is, *relying* on the judgment of others, or what one calls *prejudice* (its most dangerous form being *superstition*). The second avoids narrowness of the mind and encourages the mental habit of making a *final use* of our faculties. The third maxim of *consistent* thought is, according to Kant, "the hardest of attainment, and is only attainable by the union of both the former, and after constant attention to them has made one at home in their observance" (5:295).

Common understanding certainly can be public and ought to be held in common, but its maxims are strictly speaking not a matter of sense. If anything, these characteristics of sound understanding must be found anew as possibilities of sensing, translated into features of the aesthetic judgment: ". . . I can say that taste can with more justice be called a *sensus communis* than can sound understanding; and that the aesthetic, rather than the intellectual judgment can bear the name of a public sense." From our earlier analysis, it is possible to conjecture that the aesthetic translation of the first maxim would be indeed to trust oneself, that is, to rely on one's own pleasure as the ultimate ground in judging the object. The second maxim of judging from the standpoint of everyone else would correspond to judging with a universal voice, making one's judgment the exemplification of an idea of universal agreement. But what is the aesthetic parallel of the requirement of consistency? In what way do things hang together in our judgments if that relation cannot be understood in terms of logical consistency, which always assumes a determinant use of concepts?

To clarify this aesthetic consistency it is necessary to dwell further on Kant's use of the term 'sense.' Kant points out that in many cases we use the term 'sense' mistakenly in relation to the employment of higher faculties: ". . . there is talk of a sense of truth, a sense for propriety, for justice etc. although one surely knows, or at least properly ought to know, that these concepts cannot have their seat in a sense" (5:293). In using "sense" for these latter cases we mistake what might be a result of the use of our faculties for the character of the activity of the faculties involved. Strictly speaking, it is only in the context of aesthetic judgment that one can justifiably assess the activity of the higher faculties sensuously. There the sense, the pleasure, is not the mere result but is the criterion for the rightness of our engagement with the object.

Thus, by common *sense* Kant primarily means the "effect that mere reflection has on the mind; for then by sense we mean the feeling of pleasure" (5:295). Feeling in beauty arises by way of how one is experiencing the object. And it is that pleasurable awareness that must be construed on the model of a sense ("we want to get a look at the Object with our own eyes, just *as if* our delight depended on sensation" [5:216, my emphasis]). But pleasurable contemplation cannot be grounded on the external causality of perception. It is not, as Kant puts it, ". . . to be taken to mean some external sense, but the effect arising from the play of our powers of cognition." Sense, thus, refers to our pleasurable awareness in reflection (which is distinct from the identification of actual perceptual properties of the object). It involves the imagination in such a way that what it brings to our experience of the object comes to bear on our meaningful judgment of it. The activity of the imagination would open a space of reflection that is experienced as belonging to the object itself, thus inflecting our sense of it.

It is precisely this opening to meaning by way of the singular beautiful thing that would require some inner measure. Indeed, it would seem that the more one loosens the anchoring in actual perception, that is, the more the imagination is involved in our experience, the more there will be a threat that the movement of the mind will result in a stream of private

associations, thus losing the possibility of one's judgment being representative of universal agreement. Yet, how would we restrict the imagination
without having any pre-given concept to which it would be required to
provide something like a proportionate schematization? Common sense
is the capacity to sense the inner *systematic* relatedness of that imaginative
involvement in the object experienced.

What is the sensing of the relatedness of material of the imagination as
though it all belongs together to that which is beautiful? It might be useful here to recall the Aristotelian notion of a *sensus communis*, which accounts for the unity of the senses. The meeting point of the senses is not
a further sense that has its own mode of access to the world; rather, it is a
form of gathering of the five senses. It is not accounted for by the mere
coexistence of different properties but involves their interrelation, their
belonging together. So it is not determined solely by spatial and temporal
contiguity, by co-location (which provides at most external relation). Nor
can this relatedness be explained by way of similarity or analogy (for the
perceptual spaces have different forms or grammars) or by causality (for
we are speaking of the inner relations of perceptual spaces, not of the relation of the object to our senses). Moreover, we do not assume an intellectual essence to be the ground of the unity of the perceptual spaces. Rather,
relatedness is the coming together of heterogeneous spaces in a final form.

Kant's account of common sense, for which he also uses the Latin term
sensus communis, is in many ways continuous with Aristotle's understanding. The identity of the beautiful, *what* it is that is beautiful, is revealed by
the gathering power of beauty. Beauty can gather within itself irreducible
dimensions of meaning, thus making the beautiful thing into their meeting point. To allow beauty to be such a meeting point requires not reducing it to one register of significance (i.e., not determining it under a concept). It is a field in which heterogeneous dimensions of meaning can touch
each other, as it were in the vanishing point of the unfolding of purposiveness without purpose. Beauty draws us by drawing things together.

Interpreting common sense in this way, it becomes clear why Kant
views "common sense as the necessary condition of the universal communicability of our knowledge, which is presupposed in every logic and
every principle of knowledge that is not one of skepticism" (5:239). As we
saw Kant refers in different places to the relation between the aesthetic

judgment and "cognition in general." It is tempting to read this reference in terms of what I have called the minimalist reading of the judgment of taste, namely, as a claim that the aesthetic is precognitive. But given our understanding of common sense a different reading of its relation to cognition is possible, namely, through the idea of systematicity.

Common sense is the aesthetic dimension of systematicity. As such it would precisely address the skeptical threat that Kant raises in the introduction to the *Critique of Judgment:* "For it is quite conceivable that, despite all the uniformity of the things of nature according to universal laws, without which we would not have the form of general empirical knowledge at all, the specific variety of the empirical laws of nature, with their effects, might still be so great as to make it impossible for our understanding to discover in nature an intelligible order . . ." (5:185). Logic cannot provide any assurance that the variety of fields of experience articulated by way of their empirical laws can form a systematic interconnected order. A sense of this possibility must be given by judgment, where different aspects of experience come together and bear on each other while retaining their irreducible independence. Common sense would be the aesthetic presupposition of judgment's advance toward systematicity. In other words, judgment relies on common sense in assuring that heterogeneous meaningful phenomena can constitute an interconnected order apart from any overarching principles. Common sense would provide the aesthetic measure holding together disparate orders that as far as we know are irreducible to one another.

This elaboration of systematicity can also relate back to our use of the notion of common sense as a wisdom that takes its strength from the ordinary. The aesthetic judgment does not just point to the horizon of an ideal community of taste, but is also devoted to our common, ordinary world.[12] Beauty, like the ordinary, is open to view. There is nothing hidden in the object of beauty; rather, it is wholly present to the judge of taste. Nevertheless, this does not imply that it is meaningfully present without further ado. That is, the aesthetic judgment is precisely giving expression to what is already in plain view. In doing so one cannot rely on expert knowledge; rather, it is necessary to speak for others by relying on one's sense of what belongs together.

We might further identify this turn to the ordinary with having a measured sense of things. It is not an immediate intuition of familiarity but rather the capacity of weighing disparate aspects or giving everything its proper weight. This can be called (referring to the fundamental figure Kant uses in the fourth moment) a sense of *proportion*. For if there is something against which common sense is appealed to, it is excess of one side of our nature (usually our intellectual excesses). We also speak of exercising common sense as being sensible, meaning thereby having a sense of the balance of all sides, taking different aspects into account. Such a sense of proportion would be distinct from knowledge given by rules. For the balancing of rules cannot be a further rule. Moreover, though one can have a multitude of considerations or matters to take into account, the balance is a fine-tuned, even pointed, state. One can sense that everything is in balance without having to articulate in detail what is involved in every aspect of the matter. It is this balanced relatedness that one can sense, no matter how much meaning one brings to the beautiful and relate to it and through it.

Common sense is a sense of proportion that cannot be calculated. In common sense nothing is excessive; everything gets its right weight. It is a sense of measure exhibited by occupying a certain standpoint, by a stance toward things. It is not quite a standard against which reality is judged, as a ruler might be placed next to the object. But rather it demands placing oneself *in the midst of things* by taking everything into account. This balance of common sense is not an averaging but a sense of the world that takes beauty to be the meeting point of its dimensions. In beauty one feels at home or oriented in the world.

Part **II**

The Analytic of
the Sublime

... it is possible to recognize the dominance in the unconscious mind
of a 'repetition-compulsion' ... a compulsion powerful enough to
overrule the pleasure principle, lending to certain aspects of the mind
their daemonic character ...

—Sigmund Freud

Whereas our judgments of beauty give us hope for a hidden
harmony between our faculties and nature, the sublime brings us face to
face with the absolute worth of reason over and above nature.[1] It is the
experience of the unconditioned character of reason. This last characterization immediately raises a problem: It is Kant's understanding that human experience has conditions of possibility; that is, it is always the experience of the conditioned. So how could there be an *experience* of the
unconditioned capacity of reason? To put it paradoxically, the sublime
would be an experience of what lies beyond experience. A partial resolution of this paradox is afforded if we keep in mind that, first, the sublime
is experience in feeling rather than a perceptual access to what is beyond
experience. Second, it is our failure to present in intuition the unconditioned nature of reason that is itself felt, negatively, to present reason. Yet,
this double defense against the possibility of an intuitive presentation of
the unconditioned itself raises a new problem: How can Kant be justified
in claiming that it is *reason* that is so felt by the failure of our representational capacities? How can a feeling of failure be specific enough to determine negatively the object of the sublime experience?

There is a further difficulty in fitting the sublime into Kant's account of the aesthetic judgment. For, after reading Kant's account of the judgment of beauty, we might doubt that it is possible to square the experience of the sublime with the very idea of a reflective judgment. The question is not only how to characterize the difference between two distinct experiences in the field of aesthetics but also how the sublime could belong to aesthetics at all, at least if we start by understanding it by way of the 'Analytic of the Beautiful.' The sublime is an experience of absolute greatness or of absolute power. Of course, immensity and might have an *effect* on us, but the problem is precisely that they are too effective. The four moments of the 'Analytic of the Beautiful' emphasize the restful quality of that state of mind so that the contemplative stance becomes almost identified with the aesthetic reflective judgment. How, then, can one encompass within the space of reflective judgment the intensely moving experience of the sublime?

The problem becomes even more acute when one considers some of the contrasts Kant points to between the beautiful and the sublime: If the beautiful essentially involves purposive form revealed in the movement of the mind, the sublime arises from that which exhibits formlessness and is experienced as counter-purposive. We experience it in the face of "bold, overhanging and, as it were, threatening rocks, thunderclouds piled up the vault of heaven, borne along with flashes and peals, volcanoes in all their violence of destruction, hurricanes leaving devastation behind, the boundless ocean rising with rebellious force . . ." (5:261). The beautiful is felt in a condition of disinterest, whereas the sublime is experienced as thwarting our interests. Whereas the pleasure in the beautiful is a continuous enlivening of the play of our faculties, the sublime has an arresting aspect; it shakes us or is felt as "a momentary check of the vital forces followed at once by a discharge all the more powerful" (5:245). The sublime is an emotion rather than a reflective pleasure. It moves us in ways that only something serious and of immediate concern can move us. Nothing is left of the playfulness of the imagination so central to the judgment of taste. For it is not only nature that appears in its violent manifestations. The experience also seems to involve violence on our very faculty of presentation, violence done to our imagination. And how can doing violence to ourselves be justified even if it is in and on the imagination? How can it figure in a justification of the validity of a reflective judgment?

§1. The Mathematically Sublime

Kant suggests that there are two distinct modes of experiencing the sublime, the one having to do with magnitude, or the experience of the absolutely great in the mathematically sublime, the other with absolute power in the dynamically sublime. Since the "structure" of the experience is most developed in Kant's account of the mathematically sublime, it is to it that I will devote much of my analysis in this part.

Kant defines the mathematically sublime as what is *absolutely great*. This is further glossed as being great beyond all comparison, which does not mean that the sublime will always be judged greater than whatever we compare it with. Rather, the definition states that the sublime is *incomparably* great. It requires no comparison to establish it as such. If the very idea of estimating magnitude aesthetically were not surprising enough, it turns out that in such estimates we cannot use the basic form of measuring; namely, we cannot judge by comparison with a standard or measure. It is as though what is sublime shows itself to be absolutely great from its own ground, in itself. It is, one could say, its own standard or contains its standard within itself. This already suggests that we would have a problem finding the sublime in nature and that nothing in the external world can properly be called absolutely great. Since every corporeal body is an extensive magnitude, it is therefore measurable and comparable to any other. This is why Kant states from the very start that "the sublime, in the strict sense of the word, cannot be contained in any sensuous form, but rather concerns ideas of reason" (5:245).

Kant starts his explication of the judgment of the sublime with an account of what a magnitude is, and what could constitute an aesthetic judgment of magnitude. The understanding secures the applicability of the concept of *magnitude* to all appearances. Yet, the concept of a magnitude only tells us that something *has size*. In order to determine this size by the application of the concept of magnitude, one needs a measure unit (as it were, a ruler placed alongside the object) and a concept of number to add up the unit of measurement so as to arrive at the size of that which is measured. Such judgment will be, by definition, only of what is comparatively great and will, moreover, always be a determinant rather than a reflective judgment.

In contrast to the objective measurement provided by the understanding, the aesthetic estimation of greatness is a subjective measure provided by the imagination. Since the aesthetic standard must be universally valid, it cannot be derived from the *matter* of sensation. It is, rather, formal, that is, constituted by the very form of the activity of the imagination. The two activities of the imagination invoked by Kant to explicate the formation of the standard are apprehension and comprehension.[2] The given in intuition is always manifold. Apprehension refers to the activity of the imagination, which, can, as it were, focus on a particular area of a given manifold and treat it as one, as a unit. Now, given a unit of apprehension (which is not necessarily a specifiable part of the manifold recognized in a concept), we can start measuring the object in the imagination by adding up the unit of apprehension repeatedly. In order not to apply a concept of number, not to count, one needs to *keep the successive concatenation of the unit in mind*. This involves another activity of the imagination, that of comprehension, which allows it to retain in mind even that which is no longer perceived. The process of comprehension has nevertheless a limit, for at some point by further adding a unit we start loosing the units which were earlier concatenated. This breakdown of the imagination defined by the limit of comprehension given a unit of apprehension Kant calls the *fundamental measure of greatness* or what is *great without qualification.*

Note that the measure of greatness produced is not the unit of apprehension but is defined through the breakdown of comprehension, given such a unit. Moreover, the point of breakdown is independent of the choice of the unit of apprehension; for each such choice there will be a point of breakdown that results from putting the units together. The measure is thus *subjective*, yet its definition depends only on features of the activity of the imagination that are common to all and independent of the initial choice of unit of apprehension.

It is further important to stress that the breakdown of the imagination comes about when we attempt to give an estimate of what is *great without qualification* and not of what is sublime. As Kant warns us, "to assert without qualifications that something is great is quite a different thing from saying that it is absolutely great" (5:248). In other words, at that point we just have an aesthetic estimate of something being simply great and not yet an estimate of the sublime. Indeed, the examples that Kant gives of the emotional effects of the size of the pyramids as well as the "bewilderment, or sort of perplexity, which, as is said, seizes the visitor on first entering St. Peter's in Rome" (5:252) are not meant to exemplify the sublime but rather an aesthetic judgment of something being estimated as great.

Failing to distinguish properly between the aesthetic estimate of greatness and the judgment of sublimity is the source of many misinterpretations of Kant's account. Let me briefly lay out the structure of such common misreadings and the problems they raise, and then bring out the features of Kant's account that would avoid the difficulties. The common reading of the structure of the experience of the sublime is one that involves a break and a leap. On that model the imagination is from the very start saddled with a task that is inherently beyond its capacity, that of estimating what is boundless. When, unsurprisingly, it fails, reason is called to the rescue and shows itself equal to the task of providing an idea of the totality which the imagination failed to measure.

One can raise various difficulties with this narrative: For one thing, why would the imagination be assigned a task to which it is from the start unfit? Is it reason which demands it? And if so, wouldn't the imagination be sacrificed for the interest of reason? Instead of providing a schema of the imagination for an idea of reason, we would have a scheming of reason to bring about the failure of the imagination for the sake of its own self-aggrandizement. But this would go against a crucial feature of the aesthetic judgment, namely, that no interest is the cause of the pleasure that is aroused. Instead, there would be a determinate *end* at the basis of the pleasure and a project of reason in bringing about that end by causing the failure of the imagination. Moreover, the imagination would fail very early in the attempt to estimate the infinite. It would not even begin to rise from its dependence on the sensuous interests that guide it. In other words, there is an essential gap between the supposed breakdown of the imagination and the idea of reason, one that would require an unjustified leap to bridge, so that the former would strictly speaking not provide, even negatively, a schema for the latter. One could even wonder why it is reason that is presented by the failure of the imagination. If there is no essential connection between the acrobatics of the imagination and the idea of reason, why couldn't we argue that the failure of the imagination gives us a sense of the transcendence of God, for instance? For God would be equally unreachable by the imagination. Is Kant then merely choosing the content of the judgment of the sublime in a way that best fits his view of things?

Avoiding these problems would require clearly distinguishing the aesthetic estimate of greatness from the judgment of the sublime. A further moment is required to move from an estimate of what is great without qualification to judging the sublime. Given an estimation that something is great without qualification we can always take that which is so estimated, turn it into a new unit of apprehension, and start the process of comprehension in the imagination all over again. That this process can be repeated indefinitely is part of the judgment of sublimity. Kant describes such a movement at the end of section 26:

A tree judged by the height of man gives, at all events a standard for a mountain; and supposing this is, say, a mile high, it can serve as unit for the number expressing the earth's diameter; similarly the earth's diameter for the known planetary system; this again for the Milky way.

Kant goes on to say, ". . . Now in the aesthetic estimate of such an immeasurable whole, the sublime does not lie so much in the greatness of the number, as in the fact that in our onward advance we always arrive at proportionally greater units" (5:256). It is therefore the periodical failure of the imagination, *thus* its potential boundless advance, that is a necessary moment for the experience of the sublime. The realization of the imagination that it can go on, turning thereby all that was judged great to appear *small*, is integral to the structure of the experience. As Kant puts it:

The systematic division of the cosmos conduces to this result. For it represents all that is great in nature as in turn becoming little; or, to be more exact, it represents our imagination in all its boundlessness, and with it nature, as sinking into insignificance before the ideas of reason, once their adequate presentation is attempted. (5:257)[3]

Thus, even if the movement of the imagination is guided by reason's requirement for totality, it does not mean that the breakdown of the imagination occurs through a demand to comprehend something intrinsically over and beyond its capacity. Comprehension is invoked in an attempt to keep in mind the units of apprehension, not as a requirement to grasp the infinite. Reason might indeed point the way for taking the breakdown of comprehension so as to define a new unit of apprehension for the imagination, but in so doing it would be in line with its regulative employment. The imagination turns out to be employed in the service of reason, but in no way through reason's outstripping the bounds of its normal employment.

Yet, how would this help in judging reason to be absolutely great or to be sublime? How are we to estimate the magnitude of employments of our faculties? What is it to say that an employment or a certain capacity of a mental faculty is greater than another or that a capacity is absolutely great? The answer Kant gives is that the standard of sense that the imagination produces in estimating nature (i.e., the fundamental measure of greatness) can be used itself to measure the capacity of the imagination; we reverse the roles of measure and measured. From one point of view, then, we have the imagination measuring what is great without qualification in nature outside of us, by means of the moment of breakdown of comprehension. But this very measurement can be reversed; that is, the limit of comprehension can provide a subjective estimate of the capacity of the imagination when guided by sensuous interests. From this latter point of view each moment has a different signification. The moment of "success" for the imagination, that is, the moment of the limit of comprehension, when it achieves its task of estimating what is great, has a negative significance when what is measured is the capacity of the imagination: It shows it to be limited. The moment of "failure," that is, the moment the imagination realizes that what it estimated as great can be surpassed, is at the same time, from another perspective, a moment of realization for the imagination that *it can go on;* thus from the new point of view it is a moment that produces pleasure.[4]

Kant describes the mental movement in terms that capture the repetition and alternation of pleasure and pain involved in it:

The mind feels itself *set in motion* in the representation of the sublime in nature; whereas in the aesthetic judgment upon what is beautiful therein it is *in restful contemplation*. This movement, especially in its inception, may be compared with a vibration, i.e. with a rapidly alternating repulsion and attraction produced by one and the same Object. (5:258)

This series of repeated successes or failures, depending on the point of view one takes, *constitutes* the measure of the sublime. We have a shift from the repeated attempt of the imagination directed by sensuous interests at providing an estimate of greatness to a coming to the fore of the process's very repetitiveness, as it is itself encompassed in the mind. The alternation or repetitiveness of the process provides the sense that the imagination in its boundless advance is here driven by something that lies beyond it or beyond the sensuous interests that govern it. Invoking repetition allows us to understand better Kant's sense that the movement does violence to inner sense, to our sense of time. Indeed, comprehension turns succession into coexistence, but it is only repetition that can allow us to sense time in its potential infinity as co-present at one glance (see 5:259).

The advance of the imagination measures the capacity of our own mind by being part of it. Thus the state of mind is one that contains its standard within itself. The judgment of the sublime does not involve any external comparison between an idea of reason that is unpresentable and a presentation of the imagination. The judgment is constituted by the progress of the imagination guided by its sensuous interests. It is at the same time a progression of sensuous estimates of the power of the imagination that shows itself repeatedly, despite all enlargements of its scope, limited and partial. That repetition in the mind makes manifest a capacity, the mind's own capacity to encompass the repeated estimates. That which encompasses this progression in the mind is a capacity essentially greater than all those partial achievements of the imagination since it includes them *within itself*. Thus the state of mind presents directly, yet negatively, its own incomparable immeasurability.

Recall here Kant's claim that "it is the disposition of the soul evoked by a particular representation engaging the attention of the reflective judgment and not the object that is to be called sublime" (5:250). What is absolutely great, what is sublime, is a capacity we have, a possible *employment* of our faculties. Moreover, the reflective judgment is not *about* that disposition; rather, a disposition of *my own* mind is evoked by the movement of the imagination: "It is also evident from this that true sublimity must be sought only in *the mind of the one who judges*, not in the object of nature, the judging of which occasions this disposition in it" (5:256, my emphasis). It is not a symbolization of an idea of reason as an abstract entity that is at issue, but rather a sense of reason in the first person, as what *I* partake in, that is experienced.

This sense of a capacity of myself in and through the activity of the faculties is something we have encountered in the judgment upon beauty. But it becomes even more pronounced as a feature of the sublime. Whereas in the case of the beautiful we can speak equally of the revelation of a capacity of our mind and of the form of finality in the object, in the sublime the outer is merely the occasion for a heightened sense of self. "All that we can say is that the object lends itself to the presentation of sublimity in the mind" (5:245). The sublime has, strictly speaking, no outer object. Indeed, the experience depends on the capacity of the imagination to detach itself from each estimate and to go on. It does not remain in any bounded area of nature, nor does it dwell on any form.

This clarifies why the "content" of the judgment of the sublime is not something that is appended to the movement of the imagination. Indeed, if this is the picture we have, then it is hard to see how one can move from the experience of the frustration of the imagination to a judgment *about* the supersensible. Since, according to my interpretation, there is no content that is independent of the encompassing of the movement of the imagination in the mind, there is then no place for disagreement as to what the judgment of the sublime is about. Insofar as we follow Kant in his model of the *constitution* of the reflective judgment of the sublime, there is no doubt about its content. It is a judgment of the capacity of my own mind, my being endowed with reason.

§2. The Sublime, Morality, and Fanaticism

I want to turn now briefly to the analysis of the dynamically sublime. If the mathematically sublime had to do with a relation of the faculties when reason operated in its theoretical employment, the dynamically sublime involves reason and its relation to the imagination in the practical realm. What is then to be measured is our *capacity to act*. The sublime presents our capacity to act absolutely, not to be conditioned in our actions by sensuous interests. In other words it presents our capacity to act freely. Just as with the case of the mathematically sublime, here too we cannot measure nature's might quantitatively by way of the application of concepts. If it is to be a purely aesthetic judgment, we must find within ourselves a subjective measure for the might of nature. Nature in its power threatens our sensible interests; when we imagine the threat to incapacitate us, the feeling that is generated is *fear*. The moment of fear can serve as our subjective estimate of the might of nature.

Here too, just as in the case of the mathematically sublime, we can reverse the measurement and use the feeling to measure our mind. Fear is generated by imagining the effect of the might of nature on our capacity to act. Nature outside can thus serve to picture the vulnerability of nature within. The moment of fear can serve as an estimate of our capacity to act on our sensuous interests. What is shown in the imagination is that this capacity can always be reduced to nothing by the might of nature. But it is precisely this vulnerability that makes present to us a capacity that might have been hidden in our everyday dealings with the world. We feel the capacity to act apart from a prior interest in the end of the action. We experience negatively a capacity to *act* that is absolute. It will be our capacity to act independently of any sensuous interests, that is, freely. The affect associated with this sense of a capacity against the backdrop of fear is something Kant finds very close to the moral feeling, namely to the feeling of respect for the moral law. This similarity raises various questions concerning the "authenticity" of the experience of the sublime as well as regarding possible perversions of this experience.[5]

Consider first a problem that might be raised in regard to Kant's analysis, namely, that there is some deceit in the fact that one experiences the might of nature from a safe distance. The experience can be authentic, one might argue, only if we truly are in danger. To counter this objection Kant claims that the value of the experience

is not diminished by the fact that we must see ourselves as safe in order to be sensible of this inspiring satisfaction, in which case (it might seem), because the danger is not serious, the sublimity in our

spiritual capacity is also not to be taken seriously. For the satisfaction
here concerns only the vocation of our capacity as it is revealed to us
in such a case, just as the predisposition to it lies in our nature, while
the development and exercise of it is left to us and remains our responsibility. (5:262)

The objection turns on a confusion between the aesthetic and the practical. Truly acting requires us to overcome psychological obstacles, such
as the fear we might have in a specific situation. But sensing our capacity
to act is not actualizing that capacity. Only in the latter case is the question whether we can face our fears decisively relevant. The sublime is the
experience of a capacity, but not an achievement or actualization of that
capacity that would then testify to our developed moral character. We are
warned not to identify what is involved in acting from that absolute ground
of the will with the mere feeling of the capacity to act in that way (which
leaves us to take responsibility for our action). The confusion of the two
can lead to what Kant calls fanaticism.

Kant uses the term 'fanatic' or 'fanaticism' *(Schwärmerei)* in different
contexts—cognitive, moral, and aesthetic: "If fanaticism in its most general sense is a deliberate overstepping of the limits of human reason, moral
fanaticism is this overstepping of limits which practical pure reason sets
to mankind" (*CPR*, 5:85). In the 'Analytic of the Sublime' we learn that
such deliberate overstepping of the limits of reason involves a specific affective dimension. The aesthetic inflection of fanaticism is described as a
perversion of the experience of sublimity:

> *Fanaticism* . . . is a *delusion* that would *will some* VISION *beyond all*
> *bounds of sensibility;* i.e. would dream according to principles (rational
> raving). . . . If enthusiasm is comparable to the *delusion of sense*, fanat-
> icism may be compared to the *delusion of mind.* Of these the latter is
> least of all compatible with the sublime, for it is *profoundly* ridiculous.
> In enthusiasm, as an affection, the imagination is unbridled; in fanat-
> icism, as a deep-seated, brooding passion, it is anomalous. The first is
> a transitory accident to which the healthiest understanding is liable
> to become at times the victim; the second is an undermining disease.
> (5:275, translation modified)

In assessing the aesthetic component in what drives the fanatic we are required to consider not only Kant's transcendental psychology as it accounts for the *logic* of illusion, or the dialectic of reason, but also to engage in, as it were, transcendental psychopathology. Yet, the affective disorder of fanaticism is not limited to the field of aesthetics, but rather signals a moral problem, call it the aestheticization of morality. Certain perversions of the experience of the sublime show not only a lack of taste but also more importantly indicate a moral failing. The scope of that problem will be seen to be rather extensive and will include possibilities of aestheticization not only of the moral but also of the political domain as well.[6]

But how exactly is the fanatic's affective state a perversion of the authentic feeling of sublimity? There is an initial difficulty in relating the two insofar as we think of the experience of the sublime as a rare and transitory experience whereas fanaticism is a deliberate "deep-seated brooding passion." The latter is not just a passing affection but a fixation of the faculty of desire. The experience of the sublime is indeed rare and always restricted in duration; one cannot live at such heights of feeling.[7] But this momentariness should not be attributed to what is revealed in the experience. It presents the permanent condition of our being in the world endowed with reason. It lets us feel the uncanniness of that condition.

The true experience of the sublime is transitory insofar as it is purely negative and foregoes any positive, intuitive presentation of the transcendent. The relation to the unconditioned can be *sustained* only within morality, in terms of duty. As opposed to this, we find in fanaticism "a *delusion that would will some* VISION *beyond all the bounds of sensibility*" (5:275). The fanatic craves for a vision of the unconditioned. Fanaticism is thus the fantasy of having an intuitive, thus permanent, hold on what is revealed momentarily, and only negatively, in the experience of the sublime. This is importantly different from the case of those who merely follow their natural inclination against their better moral judgment. For something of the grandeur of the sublime remains, though displaced, in the fanatic's state of mind. The fanatic is empowered by the illusion that he can partake in the unconditioned. In the *Critique of Practical Reason* Kant calls the fanatic arrogant. His is a form of aggrandized self-love. He is flattering himself "with a spontaneous goodness of heart, needing neither spur nor bridle nor even command" (*CPR*, 5:85). Fanaticism is an entrenched disregard for human finitude. The fanatic attempts to avoid the relation to the law that is determined by duty and command. His transgression of the bounds of reason is manifested in the illusion that he can sustain a non-problematic relation to the moral law. The fanatic indulges in fantasies of *moral perfection*. Put slightly differently, the fanatic's original problem is his sense that he can intuit the ultimate grounds of the will, thereby avoiding the anxiety inherent in sustaining the infinite demand of the practical relation to the moral law.

Kant's claim that I cannot intuit the ultimate grounds of my will is sometimes seen as a claim about a possible uncertainty I would have about my motives, or a lack of transparency with regard to what really motivates me. For sure, acting at all would involve being conscious of the maxim governing my action. So is a doubt possible as to whether I adopt a maxim out of duty, rather than out of hidden interest? Insofar as we are not told what this doubt amounts to exactly, it would remain an abstract possibility that could cause some unease but no existential crisis. It would not make much difference to the phenomenology of moral consciousness.

But there is a much more basic issue at stake: When we construe the matter as one of certainty regarding ultimate motives, we retain the grammar of knowledge to relate to the will. Yet, for Kant, holding that our relation to our intelligible character is not a matter of knowledge does not mean that such character falls under the conditions of experience but we cannot know its constitution with certainty. Rather, it means that the conditions of knowledge, in particular the form of time, do not fit it at all. (Recall that Kant thinks of the experience of the sublime as doing violence to our sense of time.)

Specifically, if we think of our life as making manifest our moral character, then our finitude is tantamount to there being no point in time in which we could take our moral character to be fully determined. By this I mean that we get a sense of a moral task that can be fulfilled only in time, and no moment in one's life can provide a measure of being true to that call. The fanatic's craving for vision is an attempt to do away altogether with the tension between living in time and the timelessness of the unconditioned demand.

We would have an easier time with morality if we could intuit our moral character, as the fanatic wants it. That is, to be certain that I acted morally in a given context would show me that at bottom I do have a good character, even if in other circumstances I fail to heed the moral calling. Yet, the relation of character to morality is incapable of being divided. Relating that way to my actions, I, as it were, adopt a stance of knowledge toward the supersensible ground of the will. But the absolute inwardness of the good will implies the impossibility of relating to morality in any way other than as an infinite demand. Nothing is final, over with, or secured. Morality is not something that can be possessed.

Part III

Nature and Art

Flowers and animals that people find ugly always strike them like artefacts. "It looks like a . . ." they say. This illuminates the meaning of the words "ugly" and "beautiful."

—Ludwig Wittgenstein

It is sometimes claimed that Kant's account of beauty is fundamentally oriented toward natural beauty and gives only a secondary place to the beauty of art. Given the interpretation I have proposed of Kant's argument, particularly where it concerns the centrality of the articulation of meaning to the aesthetic judgment, I think this claim is wrong. Indeed, natural beauty might not be such as to elicit elaborate reflection, but it is only one side of the aesthetic field. Insofar as one adopts the methodological rule, that every duality presented in the *Critique of Judgment* is to be read through the prism of the mediating function of judgment, there is no room to introduce a hierarchical order into the distinction between nature and art or to take our response to natural beauty as a paradigm for what aesthetic judgment really is. Indeed, almost every issue of the 'Third Critique' is traversed by the tense coexistence of the duality of nature and art. In what follows, this duality will constitute the guideline for showing the inner logic in the development of the different topics that follow the relatively ordered treatment of the beautiful and of the sublime.

§1. The Appearance of Nature in Art

Beauty can be found either in nature or in art.[1] This, in itself, should be striking, at least if we refrain from taking the artwork to be beautiful because it imitates beautiful nature. But what then is the relation between the two? The relation of the beautiful artwork to nature is understood by Kant as a characteristic of its form: "[In] a product of art one must be aware that it is art, and not nature; yet the purposiveness in its form must still seem to be as free from all constraint by arbitrary rules as if it were a mere product of nature" (5:306). It is clear why we would have an interest in finding intelligent design in nature, but why would we want art to look as if it is nature? Isn't it too symmetrically neat to argue that "nature was beautiful, if at the same time it looked like art; and art can only be called beautiful if we are aware that it is art and yet it looks like nature" (5:306)? In particular, how can the awareness that something is art come together with its having the appearance or look of nature? What is it for something to *look like* nature, and what is it for it to be *recognized* as art?

Kant elaborates that sense of the naturalness of art in terms of the product's finality. It must appear free from artificiality, free of arbitrary or conventional rules. In other words, the object must give the sense of having an inner necessity that we identify with nature, with what admits of no choice. Yet, the characterization of nature as ordered by necessary and universal laws would not do to account for the "appearance of nature" in art. For laws are formulated by way of a plurality of objects whose behavior they describe. And in the case of beauty we need to characterize the appearance of nature in the singular object rather than in the lawful behavior of objects in general. Should we then conceive of the appearance of a natural object on the model of the purposive structure of the organism? That is, would Kant advocate an organicist conception of the work of art?

Maybe, before asking what it is for something manmade to appear natural, we need to inquire what it is in the beauty of nature that makes its naturalness essential to its beauty. That is, when do we have in the experience of *beauty in nature* a sense of the natural provenance of the object? We have of course various ways of knowing that something is natural rather than artificial, of assessing that it could not have come to existence unless by generation from another natural being. But this is not the same as experiencing its naturalness as being inseparable from the aesthetic judgment on it. Natural beauty is not just beauty that happens to be found in nature; rather, it is beauty that has in it something of what nature is for us.

The characterization of the impact of natural beauty, of the belonging of beauty to nature, is most evident in Kant's discussion of the interests we have in the beautiful. Though we judge beauty disinterestedly, we have interests in the *existence* of beauty in the world. Put differently, we have interests in the possibility of judging disinterestedly. Such higher-order interests are of two kinds, empirical and intellectual, and they differ from each other in part in terms of the origin of their object, whether it is natural or artificial. So, for instance, it is of interest to us that there are works of art in the world, for their existence fosters communication, the formation of a community of taste. Their judgment involves communicability, and while we should not judge for the sake of others and the communication with them, such sociability may develop out of the judgments of a work of art. Since clearly works of art allow more meaningful complexities of articulation than the beauty of nature, thus occasion more social exchange, the interest in sociability is primarily an interest in the existence of beauty in art. But for Kant, marking that interest as empirical implies that it is of a lesser order than the intellectual interest in beauty. That latter we can have only in the existence of beauty in nature.

It can become for us important to the highest degree that there is beauty in nature. Why should there be, after all? Can we find a reason for it in the natural world? Certainly, nature as mechanism gives no explanation for the presence of beauty in it. But it is important to add that neither does the contemplation of nature as a purposive system. For this reason, the very existence of beauty in nature can be a higher, *moral* interest of ours. In the next part I will describe more specifically the character of this interest. But here what I want to stress is that our aesthetic sense of the provenance of beauty from nature is evident primarily in these cases in which the dissociation of the beautiful form of the natural product from a possible system of natural ends makes the mere existence of it in nature striking to us. It has no reason to be there. In other words, we are dealing with cases where the consideration of the beautiful form, in all its inner complexity, is not the main concern. It is as though the mere existence of beauty is enough. Therefore, the simplest beauty that is found profusely dispersed on the surface of the earth is the one that will have the highest significance for us.[2]

One might say that what is striking is precisely that beauty is there, so to speak, in itself, without a ground. We are elated by the sense that something that is just there is, for no reason, still so singularly adapted to us that it lets us enjoy the freedom of our own mind. We then sense that nature itself gives us a hint of its possible harmony with our *highest* human ends.[3] It is crucially only something that has nature as its origin that can produce this peculiar interest. We would not be so surprised by the harmony of our faculties with an artificial product. It would not have *that* higher significance for us.

Kant gives the example of a "jovial host" who

has played a trick on the guests with him on a visit to enjoy the country air, and has done so to their huge satisfaction, by hiding in a thicket a rogue of a youth who (with a reed or rush in his mouth) knew how to reproduce [the nightingale's] note so as to hit off nature to perfection. (5:302)

What is of interest in such simple and free beauty as the song of the nightingale at night is not any elaborate form, but rather its very presence in nature. This makes it an intellectual interest in beauty that is freely provided by nature. The artificial reproduction, even if it *appears* natural and imitates the song of the nightingale perfectly, would completely thwart that interest.

We are now in a position to return to our original question and ask what it would be for a work of art to have the appearance of nature. Following our analysis of the intellectual interest in the beautiful in nature, I would argue that although we can recognize that the work of art is produced by human artifice, it must have to it, or in it, something that has the character of the *mere existence* of beautiful nature. That is, we must not think of it as imitating the different forms of natural beauty, but rather as having the appearance of something existing for its own sake, being there with no reason and for no reason. It must even appear not to be made for a beholder.[4] But how would the work of art appear to exist for itself, as though completely self- enclosed and detached from an order of reasons? What is it, in the work, that gives that appearance?

I have developed in discussing the second moment of 'The Analytic of the Beautiful' the dimension of singularity intrinsic to the judgment of taste in terms of the consideration of the beautiful as an idea-like totality. It is with respect to this dimension that we must think of how the work of art presents us with the face of natural beauty. This might be surprising insofar as for Kant ideas are precisely what is not realized in nature. Yet, as the discussion of the intellectual interest in the beautiful shows, mere nature can relate to the idea, and conversely the sense of the unity of the idea can be what presents in art the natural as such. Insofar as the beautiful thing is considered as a totality, as an idea, it has no exterior. It is one with itself; it exists for its own sake. This being essentially one is the source of its appearing free of arbitrary rule or conventions; it gives the sense that nothing in it is the product of choice. (This is sometimes put incorrectly as the claim that in a work of art every detail is important or is exactly where it ought to be. But this would be to assume that every detail was chosen and decided, and would therefore not express the sense that choice is left out of the picture.)

Now, this self-enclosed character of art is something of an illusion. For no sensible object can be the realization of an idea. As will become clear, that dimension of semblance is inherent to the aesthetic. But even so, the question remains, how we are to think of the possibility of endowing an object which is manmade with the appearance of the self-enclosed character of natural beauty, making it seem like the self-contained completeness of the idea? Is it a technique of art that can produce such an appearance?

Before suggesting the solution to this question, I want to elaborate the other side of this delicate balance Kant forms between art and nature, namely, consider how the recognition that something is art is in turn essential to its beauty. Kant gives a simple example of what it is to be aware that something is art even when found in nature: "If, as sometimes happens, in a search through a bog, we light on a piece of hewn wood, we do not say it is a product of nature but of art. Its producing cause had an end in view to which the object owes its form " (5:303). The problem with extending this example to the recognition of the artfulness of the work of art is that such awareness of the artificiality of the product would remain wholly external to the aesthetic judgment or to the appreciation that it is beautiful. Yet, Kant seems to want to claim that part of what is involved in calling art beautiful is the simultaneous recognition of its being art and its having the appearance of nature.

The awareness that something is art is essential to our judgment of its beauty. Art should not dissimulate itself, that is, hide its provenance as art and disguise itself as mere nature. It does not seek to trick one to believe something is nature when in fact it is manmade. The issue is further not the representation of nature to such a degree of perfection as to provoke the admiration of achieving something looking exactly like nature by artificial means. As though our awareness that human doing is involved would be summed up in the astonishment at the capacity to make something so naturelike as to almost deceive us concerning its provenance.

That which is artificial yet part of the aesthetically significant appearance of the work of art can be identified by Kant's reference to the rules that are always part of it. They are the conventional aspect of the work, its academic dimension, the transmittable dimension of art learned in schools, that which expresses the character of a specific period in art. These include the medium, the style, the genre, the technique, and so on. Indeed, wouldn't the awareness that something is art be captured by the recognition that it is a painting, a piece of music, a sculpture or that it has a sonata form or that it is of the impressionist school?

Assuming this aspect to be essential to the work of art, to be what is involved in the recognition that it is art, we need to ask ourselves what would then be the relation of the natural appearance of the work to *this* conventional aspect? Do we need to distinguish two wholly separate moments, the first being the recognition of the art-character of the work, and the second its natural appearance? But in that case the art character, the awareness of the conventions, would thwart the very possibility of an appearance of nature, which must be free of all conventions. Rather, we should say that the work of art shows the possibility of finding nature in and through the limitations of the conventions. A successful work of art will relate to the conventions in such a way as to show that within the space of their constraints a further step can be taken that is not determined by the preexisting rules. To put it simply, what is significant is precisely the realization that nature can appear *within* human making, not merely apart from it.

§2. The Nature of Genius

In all the preceding considerations, we might still be skirting the main issue and the fundamental tension that guides Kant's account of the relation of nature and art. The work of art is made and nature is not made. Art is not nature. What is made must have a *rule* of its making. This is analytic or belongs to our concept of what it is for something to be made. But our judgment of taste cannot be based on rules. How, then, is a work of art, a human product that elicits aesthetic judgment possible? One solution would be to distinguish the fact of the matter about the work from the state of mind of the judge of taste. As though the judge of taste does not take into account the rule that in fact is at the ground of the work or is unaware of it, and this unawareness is the condition of the possibility of his passing an aesthetic judgment. But wouldn't this turn the aesthetic judgment into a make-believe, the "as-if" too much of a self-deception? There would in fact be an answer why the work has the qualities it has, only we would put ourselves in the position of ignoring it.

This dilemma can be rephrased by reference to the artist. For if a work is a making, it must have a maker. And the maker would be the one who gives form to the work, that is, makes a product that by definition must be based on a rule. Does the maker know the rule to make the product, and would it only be the judge of taste that is unaware of the intention of the artist and would thereby be capable of engaging in a judgment of taste? Is the sense of the inexhaustibility of the beautiful, manifest in the purposiveness without purpose of the state of mind of the judge of taste, ultimately the result of the maker hiding well enough the rule that served to craft the object? Kant's resolution of this tension will lead us deeper into the relation between nature and art in the 'Third Critique.'

It is by introducing the concept of genius that Kant explains away the dilemma of the work of art. Genius is that which provides the rule in art. But genius is precisely that capacity which can never be lucid about itself. At the most fundamental level genius does not know what it is doing. The rule according to which genius creates is ultimately referred to something at work in the person of genius, yet belonging to nature. Genius is possible only as a gift of nature, as a talent, or, to put it more strongly, through genius nature gives the rule to art: "*Genius* is the talent (natural endowment) which gives the rule to art. Since talent, as an innate productive faculty of the artist, belongs itself to nature, we may put it this way: *Genius* is the innate mental aptitude *(ingenium) through which* nature gives the rule to art" (5:307). Thus we are led from the initial understanding that the work of art must wear the appearance of nature to a stronger claim that the work of art truly *contains nature* through the agency of genius.

One might misunderstand Kant's claim if one limits the role of nature to providing a nondeterminate capacity that the genius is born with. As though nature is responsible for a certain constitution of the individual. It would be wrong to think of genius as analogous to, say, being gifted with certain bodily qualities. For, even though an athlete has been endowed with particularly long legs by nature, we would not say that a rule belonging to nature is realized in the results achieved on the running track. Kant doesn't just trace the creation to an indeterminate capacity of the individual but takes the work of art to give body to a rule belonging to nature. Indeed, "nature prescribes the rule through *genius*, not to science but to art" (5:308). It is the rule *of the work* which is nature (just as one would speak of a law of nature in science). This is not to say that such a rule of nature would be visible immediately. Initially, it might be recognized only as the appearance of nature. But that appearance holds within itself the potential to be translated into a rule for all. Envisaging such a possibility requires recognizing the inner connection between genius and taste.

Indeed, if the creator "cannot of its own self excogitate the rule according to which it is to effectuate the product," if we do not have the authority of the creator as to the inner order of its creation, how would we distinguish between the original, which lacks any rule (what Kant calls "original nonsense"), and true products of genius? Kant's solution is to argue that genius is recognized by the way it can provide a gathering point or standard for taste: "Since there may also be original nonsense, its products must at the same time be models, i.e. be *exemplary;* and consequently, though not themselves derived from imitation, they must serve that purpose for others, i.e. as a standard or rule of estimating" (5:308).

The originality-lacking self-consciousness of genius becomes the condition of there being judgments of taste in art (i.e., judgments without a pregiven rule), and taste, on the other hand, becomes the condition of possibility of the realization of the work of genius (i.e., of the unfolding of the meaning of that originality). One might find the two combined in one person, but strictly speaking what opens up here is a temporal dimension that is internal to the elaboration of meaning in the work. The natural rule underlying art is realized over time in the free play of criticism that has in view the idea of universal agreement. We might indeed find in the consciousness of this temporal unfolding of meaning a way to reformulate the fact that beauty is not reducible to determinate properties of objects. The work of art is not an object but rather a *place* in which meaning unfolds over time according to the peculiar dynamics of the aesthetic sphere.[5]

To put it more provocatively perhaps, there is no work of art which is solely the making of genius. It is equally realized in its meaning by taste (or criticism). It is only insofar as that rule of nature is not explicit that there is room left for the work of taste, for expressing the meaning inherent in the work. Such lack of explicitness should not be understood merely as a problem of knowledge. The inner order of the work is not there, in actual properties of the work, awaiting taste to come and recognize it. One might speak of taste realizing the inner meaning of the work, if realization is understood both as a recognition and as a making real.[6]

§3. Nature in Culture

One could elaborate the presence of nature in art and the special temporality of its unfolding by arguing that the work of art has a *life* to it. Its aliveness is manifest not only in its source in nature given voice by genius but also in the changes it can undergo through, for instance, criticism.[7] Criticism would keep it alive and, so to speak, growing in meaning. To speak of the life of the work of art is indeed a way to conceive of it as manifesting the character of nature (though it is distinct from the natural end or organism, which is discussed in the second part of the *Critique of Judgment*). In order to grasp the justification for this use of the notion of life in relation to a work of art and ask what kind of life is being considered here, it would be useful to trace again the transformations this notion undergoes in the first part of the *Critique of Judgment* and relate it briefly to the considerations of natural teleology in its second part.

Recall that Kant opens the first moment of the 'Analytic of the Beautiful' by considering what is implied by the idea that the judgment of taste is *aesthetic*. The inherent dependence of judgment on feeling is related from the very start to the notion of life: ". . . the representation is referred wholly to the subject and what is more to its feeling of life—under the name of the feeling of pleasure or displeasure" (5:204). We would readily admit that only living beings can feel pleasure and pain, but Kant further calls pleasure and pain the feeling *of* life. Kant speaks of the feeling of life as "a feeling which the Subject has of itself and of the manner in which it is affected by the representation" (5:204). He understands the feeling of life identified in the aesthetic judgment in terms of a lively movement of the mind, that is, in terms of a movement of our faculties that has finality to it without a determinate end. "The beautiful is directly attended with a feeling of the furtherance of life" (5:244).

The notion of life reappears when Kant considers the work of art as a product of genius. The life in a work refers to its animating principle, its soul or spirit:

> Spirit *(Geist)* in an aesthetic sense signifies the animating principle in the mind. But, that whereby this principle animates the soul *(Seele)*—the material which it employs for this purpose—is that which purposively sets the mental powers into motion, i.e. into a play which is self-maintaining and which strengthens those powers for such an activity. (5:313, translation modified)

Spirit is not a further faculty of the mind, invoked so as to account for genius, over and above the imagination and the understanding. Rather, genius can endow the material of the work with the capacity for animating our faculties in judging it. In further characterizing this capacity Kant writes that it

> is nothing else than the faculty of presentation of *aesthetic ideas*; But, by an aesthetic idea, I mean that representation of the imagination that induces much thinking though, yet without the possibility of any determinate thought, i.e. concept being adequate to it, and which language, consequently, can never get quite on level terms with or render completely intelligible.—It is easily seen that an aesthetic idea is the counterpart (pendant) of an *idea of reason*, which is conversely, a

concept to which no *intuition* (representation of the imagination) can be adequate. (5:313, translation modified)

One should not confuse an aesthetic idea with an intuitive illustration of a concept. The aesthetic idea must have in itself something corresponding to the inexhaustibility of the relation of the rational idea to the phenomenal world, something of its regulative character. The aesthetic idea *occasions much thinking*, and that is how it is shown to be inexhaustible. In other words, it is only insofar as taste responds in reflection to the rich material that the genius has gathered in the work of art that the latter can be called an aesthetic idea.

With the recognition of the complex inner relations between work of art, genius and taste we come to consider the human form of life that encompasses these terms, or what we also call, culture. The peculiar temporality of the sphere of the beautiful revealed in addressing the dichotomy of the natural and the artificial provides us with something of a scheme for the dynamics of culture. The relation of nature and art in the context of the constitution of society through culture is taken up in Kant's final reflections on the aesthetic, which treat of the methodology of taste. The role of taste is initially posed by reference to the problem of the emergence of society and the necessity of bringing a people under the authority of law:

There was an age and there were nations in which the active impulse toward a social life *regulated by laws*—what converts a people into a permanent community—grappled with the huge difficulties presented by the trying problem of bringing freedom (and therefore equality) into union with constraining force (more that of respect and dutiful submission than of fear). And such must have been the age, and such the nation that first discovered the art of reciprocal communication of ideas between the more cultured and ruder sections of the community and how to bridge the difference between the amplitude and refinement of the former and the natural simplicity of the latter—in this way hitting upon that mean between high culture and the modest worth of nature, that forms for taste also, as a sense common to all mankind, that true standard which no universal rules can supply. (5:355)

In thinking of the constitution of a shared culture out of nature, one should avoid the simplistic model of nature being a substratum which human making is gradually overtaking. There are two threats in the process of constitution of culture. The one would be the resilience of brute nature, the second would be too much refinement, to the point of utter artificiality, taste becoming a mere social sense.[8] If Kant's moral philosophy is read mostly as emphasizing the first problem, his deep appreciation of Rousseau would be enough for us to realize his recognition of the second threat. Kant is not only concerned with taming rude nature, but also takes taste to be true to the "modest worth of nature," to "natural simplicity." The significance of the natural in art, seen from that perspective is not exhausted by having the work of art wear the appearance of nature. Nor is it required for explaining the productive capacity of genius. Rather, the claim is that through taste nature can become part of our sense of community, thereby avoiding taste being taken over by artificial sociability. Taste must remain true to the innocence of nature and allows it to be a force in the constitution of culture. We might say that the work of art teaches us that nature is always there, always available to put to shame our artificial excesses.

The relation of nature to culture can also be elaborated if we turn our attention to the second part of the *Critique of Judgment*. The account of teleology is initially devoted to the consideration of the organism, of natural ends, or to the understanding of the internal purposive organization of a living being. But this account is extended as Kant moves from the consideration of internal ends to that of external ends that allow us to judge how one being serves as a means for another's survival. The consideration of external ends further leads Kant to ask whether nature can also be considered as a system of ends complete in itself or one that could be said to have an ultimate end.

In considering such a system of ends Kant raises the worry that the direction of purposiveness cannot be determined when remaining solely with natural ends. How are we, for instance, to decide between the following two options: Is the vegetal kingdom a means for the herbivores and these in turn a means for the carnivores, and finally would we place man as the master of nature that can take all of the creatures of nature as means for his subsistence? Or maybe the herbivores are there only as a means to limit the luxurious growth of the vegetal kingdom and the carnivores to limit the overpopulation of the herbivores, and finally man, insofar as he destroys nature, would similarly be *a mere means* to restrict the overabundance of nature. Nothing in the order of natural ends could decide between these two systematic orderings. Nature can have an ultimate end in man only insofar as man has a side that is *beyond* nature, only if we relate nature as a whole to the deployment of man's rational capacities.

But what in man is to be considered as the ultimate end of nature as a whole? To refer to man's moral existence as the ultimate end of nature would be to aim to high. Nothing natural can have from its own ground the moral as an ultimate aim. A further answer that would suggest itself is happiness, when that is not understood merely as the satisfaction of natural needs but rather as involving an idea of a harmonious fulfillment of all aspects of our conditioned practical reason. But Kant points out that happiness is too vague and indeterminate an idea in man, so that "even if nature were to be completely subjected to his will it could still assume no determinate universal and fixed laws at all by means of which to correspond with the unstable concept and thus with the end that each arbitrary sets for himself" (5:430).

Since no contentful notion of an ultimate end can be consistently characterized, Kant turns to a formal characteristic, namely, the aptitude and skill man would have for all sort of ends for which he would use nature (external and internal). In other words, culture is the ultimate end of nature. Culture is the development of man's capacity for any natural end, the aptitude for setting ends in relation to his natural side in general. It is here that the account of teleology relates back to the aesthetic and to the fundamental role of the cultivation of taste:

> Fine arts and the sciences, if they do not make man morally better, yet, by conveying a pleasure that admits of universal communication and by introducing polish and refinement into society make him civilized. Thus they do much to overcome the tyrannical propensities of sense, and so prepare man for a sovereignty in which reason alone shall sway. (5:433)

The highest manifestation of this cultivation of the capacity for purposes in general will be our capacity to judge purposively without purpose, that is, it will be found in the aesthetic. Nature has culture as its ultimate end, and culture is true to the simplicity of nature by the life it reveals at the heart of the work of art.

§4. Beauty's Semblance

The duality of nature and what lies beyond it is also at work in Kant's discussion of the dialectic of aesthetic judgment. As is the case in the other two Critiques, the unrestricted deployment of our faculties can lead to an antinomy. One side of the antinomy of taste is stressing the natural character of taste. It is expressed in commonplace views concerning taste, such as "Every one has his own taste" and "There is no disputing about taste." The other side of the antinomy is stressing the intellectual side of taste and can just as commonly be recognized in the view that while there is no dispute (argument or proof) in matters of taste, there is clearly debate or contention. And the very possibility of such debate assumes the possibility of constituting agreement by way of our concepts, over and above our natural reactions. More precisely, the two sides of the antinomy would be formulated as follows:

1. *Thesis.* The judgment of taste is not based upon concepts, for, if it were, it would be open to dispute (decision by means of concepts).
2. *Antithesis.* The judgment of taste is based on concepts, for otherwise, despite diversity of judgment, there could be no room even for contention in the matter (a claim of the necessary agreement of others with this judgment).

The solution of the antinomy shows the possibility of holding the truth of both thesis and antithesis, so long as the thesis is understood as asserting that no determinant use of concepts for knowledge is part of aesthetic experience and the antithesis is understood as claiming that any use of concepts relates itself solely to the supersensible ground, or ties itself immediately to an *idea* of agreement:

All contradiction disappears, however, if I say: The judgment of taste does depend upon a concept (of a general ground of the subjective finality of nature for the power of judgment), but one from which nothing can be cognized in respect of the Object, and nothing proved, because it is in itself indeterminable and useless for knowledge. Yet, by means of this very concept it acquires at the same time validity for everyone (but with each individual, no doubt, as a singular judgment immediately accompanying his intuition): because its determining ground lies perhaps in the concept of what may be regarded as the supersensible substrate of humanity. (5:340)

The dialectic of aesthetic judgment precisely brings out what this study has repeatedly considered, namely, the way in which concepts can be involved without being put to use determinately. This is possible by invoking the relation of conceptual reflection to the idea of the supersensible. But note an important difference between the resolution of the antinomy of taste and that of the dynamical antinomies of the 'First Critique.' In the latter case as well the distinction between the phenomenal and the noumenal is the basis of the resolution of the antinomies. But whereas the idea of the supersensible ground plays no part in the cognitive judgments of the phenomenal world, in the case of the aesthetic judgment, the idea is *internalized* into the making of the judgment itself. In other words, it is precisely the movement of the mind in judgment that indicates that we speak with a universal voice, that we have the idea of universal agreement in view. But, since the idea cannot be truly realized in phenomena, it is as though something of the order of semblance is found to be internal to the phenomenon of beauty.

Beauty's semblance is sometimes expressed by saying that it is merely a matter of how things appear rather than a manifestation of what they truly are, of their essence. Remember that for Kant, the aesthetic, though treated in the critical philosophy, does not constitute a further realm beyond those of nature and freedom. This is stated clearly in the introduction, as judgment is denied any proper domain of objects over which it is legislative. It is to be conceived as a mediating field between nature and freedom. From the standpoint of each of these two realms, the judgment upon the beautiful will appear to lack something essential to our assessments of reality. In comparison to our knowledge of nature, the judgment of taste will be found lacking in conceptual determination. In comparison to the decisive determination of our will, it will also be found deficient in

the seriousness and commitment required to motivate action. What is ex-
tolled as the spirit of the rich and restful free play of our faculties in the
aesthetic is liable to appear from these standpoints in less favorable light.
It would be seen as letting into our experience of the world, postpone-
ment, ambiguity, and evasiveness. To put it in terms of an expression that
often recurs in Kant's account of judgment: Our aesthetic judgments
would have an "as if" quality to them. But in Kant's account the ontologi-
cal deficiency of beauty, its peculiar irreality, is translated into the very
unique advantage of the field of judgment. It is precisely its lack of ultimate reality that allows the aesthetic to function as a mediation between
nature and freedom.

One can also speak here of the mediation between the intelligible world
and the phenomenal world, that is of the way aesthetic judgment allows us
to sense the attraction of the idea in the phenomenal. An extreme possibility of elaborating this mediation between the infinite and the finite, as
well as the complex relation of the natural and the artificial, emerges if we
now turn our attention to the way the "as if" character of judgment is evident in the statement of the principle of reflection upon nature. For that
principle asks us to conceive of nature as if it were art, the product of design, albeit of a peculiar sort:

> As universal laws of nature have their ground in our understanding,
> which prescribes them to nature (though only according to the uni-
> versal concept of it as nature), particular empirical laws must be re-
> garded, in respect of that which is left undetermined in them by
> these universal laws, according to a unity such as they would have if
> an understanding (though it be not ours) had supplied them for the
> benefit of our cognitive faculties, so as to render possible a system of
> experience according to particular natural laws. (5:180)

Kant is quick to point out that this principle does not imply the existence of such an intellect that makes nature for our benefit: "for it is only
the reflective judgment which avails itself of this idea as a principle for the
purpose of reflection and not for determining anything" (5:180). We do
not assume the existence of such an intellect, but we nevertheless might
still have to imagine or have an idea of what it would be for nature to be

created for the benefit of our faculties, even only in order to guide judgment. What is it, otherwise, for reflective judgment to "avail itself of the idea" of such an intellect? How elaborate is the "as if" in this limit case?

Imagining an understanding like ours, only stronger, would not do. Certainly we must conceive of an understanding that originates nature, a *creative* understanding. But then again, is it an intellect which creates the world as a system of mechanical causality all the way down to the most particular laws of phenomena? Or is it an intellect for which the world is a purposive, systematic unity? Or is there yet a further way to think of the world beyond that very dichotomy between the mechanical and the purposive, that is, to conceive of that very distinction to be something pertaining to the character of *our* intellect?

To follow that last possibility would be to understand how the distinction between the mechanistic and the teleological is an outcome of our intellect being a discursive one, essentially involving both intuitions and concepts. This requires us to enter into sections 76 and 77 of the *Critique of Judgment*, which are among the most influential and definitely the most obscure sections of the work. As the title of section 77 makes clear Kant wishes to consider "the special character of the human understanding, by means of which the concept of a natural end is possible for us" (5:405). In these sections, Kant attempts to explicate the necessity, for us human beings, of viewing the world both in terms of mechanism as well as teleology by contrast with another intellect, for which no such distinction exists.

This other understanding is the one which we are to imagine in the formulation of the principle of reflective judgment. We are asked there to conceive of an understanding that is not discursive or which would not require concepts to immediately and fully cognize the world in its unity. It would be an intuitive intellect (though not one for which intuition is sensible). We cannot do with intuition alone or always require concepts provided by the understanding to synthesize the manifold of intuition. Our understanding always starts from parts and synthesizes them into a higher unity by way of concepts. The fundamental character of an intuitive understanding is, on the contrary, the way it thinks by way of the primacy of the intuitive whole to its parts. We might be able to understand what it would be for the whole to be prior to its parts by referring ourselves to the practical realm. In acting we have from the start an idea of what we ultimately want, for which we determine the means to best achieve it in given conditions. But such primacy of the whole over its parts requires for us the *concept* of an end. It is in no way the intuitive primacy of the whole assumed to belong to the intuitive understanding.

It might seem pointless to follow further on such speculations, especially as it is unclear what their bearing on aesthetics would be. But maybe beauty is precisely such as to allow us to touch even upon such a limit case, and make it present to us in experience? In Part IV of this study, I will discuss two extremes of the aesthetic field that will be seen to involve what one might call an aesthetics of the intuitive understanding. They are the ideal of beauty and the beauty of color.

Extremes of Judgment

Beautiful is what is at once charming and sublime.
—Friedrich Schlegel

It can hardly be disputed that form is central to Kant's account of aesthetics. But the structure of bridging at work in his construction of the field suggests the possibility of extremes in which the very idea of form will be problematized. I want in the present part to turn my attention to *content*, as it comes into play in two opposite extremes of Kant's account: his discussion of the ideal of beauty on the one hand and of color on the other. It will be seen that these extremes are also limit cases in relation to another fundamental distinction in the *Critique of Judgment*, that between the beautiful and the sublime. They are the cases in which one could say that the beautiful touches upon the sublime, call them the "almost sublime." Each of them will, as I suggested, give us a hold on the limit notion of an intuitive understanding and its manifestation in aesthetics.

§1. The Ideal of Beauty

The notion of the ideal plays a role in every part of the critical philosophy as well as in the doctrine of virtue, the religion, and even in Kant's metaphysics of nature.[1] Ideas provide a horizon of systematic unity and completeness to experience, which is in no way realized in experience. They are regulative with respect to the advance of our knowledge. The ideal can be said to be even more distant from experience than the idea. It is the idea conceived of as realized not merely *in concreto* but also *in individuo*, as an individual being. The distinction between idea and ideal is importantly that between a focal point for our advance defined in terms of form and one determined in relation to a maximum of content. The ideal is therefore to be conceived not as a primal concept but rather by way of the singularity characteristic of the intuitive, as a primal *image*, an *Urbild*—or archetype. Needless to say, both idea and ideal according to Kant can only be regulative for us, but they are regulative in different ways. The intuitive singularity of the ideal inflects the way we conceive of its unattainability as well as of our striving toward it.[2]

Even though ideals are not objectively present and can be improperly reified (thus the ideal of knowledge is discussed in the dialectic of the 'First Critique'), Kant argues that they are not "figments of the brain"; they have a proper use and can serve as standards of judgment to measure the degree to which a particular is adequate to an idea: "As the idea gives the *rule*, so the ideal in such cases serves as the *archetype* for the complete determination of the copy." The term 'ideal' thus belongs broadly speaking to the register of judgment in which we encounter various ways in which the concrete presents the universal. It is part of a family of terms such as the 'example,' the 'schema,' the 'exemplary,' the 'paradigmatic,' the 'type,' the 'model,' the 'prototype,' the 'standard,' and the 'archetype.' It is important to clearly distinguish the different grammars of these terms. Consider, for instance, the contrast between the function of the moral ideal for judgment and the type of moral judgment discussed in *The Critique of Practical Reason*. In both cases we have an issue of judgment that concerns the relation of a particular to what cannot be wholly embodied in appearance.

The type of the moral law is what allows judging whether a specific maxim of action falls under the moral law. Since we can have no intuitive schema of an idea, the type of moral judgment is analogical—it is the form of the law of nature used as an analogue in experience for the universality of the moral law. This type is already implicitly embedded in the famous formulation of the categorical imperative: "Act in such a way that you can will the maxim of your action to be a universal law of nature."

What is at stake in the ideal of morality is different; it does not concern a specific action but rather involves a concrete and individual organization of *character*, presented by way of certain thick moral concepts. It is an ideal of virtue that makes us sense our limitations:

> Virtue, and with it human wisdom in its entire purity, are ideas. But the sage (of the Stoics) is an ideal, i.e. a human being who exists merely in thoughts, but who is fully congruent with the idea of wisdom. Thus just as the idea gives the *rule*, so the ideal in such a case serves as the *original image* for the thoroughgoing determination of the copy; and we have in us no other standard for our actions than the conduct of this divine human being, with which we can compare ourselves, judging ourselves and thereby improving ourselves, even though we can never reach the standard. (A569/B597)[3]

Now, even though Kant characterizes the ideal as a primal image, by way of the singularity of intuitive content, he in no way wants it to be associated with the products of the imagination of artists and novelists: "to try to realize the ideal in an example, i.e., in appearance, such as that of the sage in a novel, is not feasible, and even has about it something nonsensical and not very edifying" (A570/B598). Indeed, Kant adds, the ideal should be distinguished from a "representation such as painters and physiognomists profess to carry in their heads, and which they treat as being an incommunicable shadowy image of their creations or even of their critical judgments" (A570/B598). In other words, beauty has no ideal. This is far from surprising, for, at this stage at least, Kant does not have a place for aesthetics in the critical philosophy.

As aesthetics becomes a cornerstone of the critical treatment of the power of judgment, the notion of an ideal serving as an archetype for judgment must also be reconceived. Thus, Kant introduces in *The Critique of Judgment* an ideal for beauty "that rests, not upon concepts, but upon the presentation—the faculty of presentation being the imagination" (5:232). Such an ideal, the human figure, insofar as it is "the visible expression of moral ideas that govern man inwardly," functions as an archetype for "everything that is an object of taste, or that is an example of critical taste, and even of universal taste itself" (5:232).

Even if we accept that aesthetic judgment is entirely consistent with a certain deployment of meaning, trying to account for an ideal of beauty raises extremely complex issues in Kant's aesthetics. I will list them briefly to provide an initial orientation of my discussion of the details of Kant's account. In the first place Kant mostly emphasizes the freedom from rules of the judgment of beauty, whereas the ideal seems to provide something of a determinate measure for beauty. How can judgments of beauty lack rules, yet have a standard? Second, the ideal of beauty is not a product of reason. It is an ideal that must be presented by the imagination. Yet, to truly be a standard, the ideal must be a "determinate image," not merely "a blurred sketch drawn from diverse experiences" (A570/B598). How can the imagination, especially assuming its playfulness in beauty, realize that maximal determination? Third, an ideal is a determination of content. Indeed, it is the beauty of a specific subject matter, namely, the human figure insofar as it expresses moral character. But how can such content be singled out in an aesthetic of form? Fourth, the ideal is not merely presented as the inspiration or muse for the creative genius but rather is to function as a standard of taste. Indeed, it is not just a model for the estimation of the beauty of the human figure; rather, Kant thinks of it as an archetype of *taste* as such, a standard for "universal taste itself." How would the human figure then be a measure in our judgments of beauty at large? Fifth, wouldn't the introduction of the moral register into aesthetics be wholly unjustified in terms of Kant's own account of beauty? Wouldn't it constitute an ideological framing of what was supposed to be the essentially free and imaginative character of the beautiful? Finally, while the ideal of beauty is the expression of moral character in the human figure, it cannot be a fully positive manifestation of the moral idea in the field of experience. How can the ideal be made intuitively present to us in works of arts, say, without having aesthetic fanaticism or an aestheticization of the moral?

Kant begins his account by considering the way in which the notion of the ideal of beauty has been traditionally approached in treatises in aesthetics, namely, in terms of the status of classical art. The first prerequisite for something to serve as a standard or model for judgment is its unalterability.[4] Considering the stability over time required of models, one might be tempted to identify them with classical works of the past. They have behind them, as Kant writes, "the accord, so far as possible, of all ages and nations" (5:232). Moreover, the fact that these works are no more part of their original form of life or that the form of life in which they were created has died away makes for a further stability in their meaning. This is especially true, as Kant points out, for literature, whose models must be composed in a dead language, one not affected by the transformations of meaning inevitable in a living tongue.

But the agreement over works of classical antiquity is something that must be considered from Kant's perspective as contingent, as empirical agreement. The exemplary works of the past can at most be viewed as prototypes that have themselves the true ideal in view. Thus Kant writes that ". . . the highest model, the archetype of taste, is a mere idea, which each person must beget in his own consciousness. . . . While not having this ideal in our possession we still strive to beget it in us" (5:232). It is crucial then that the ideal is something the judge of taste is to strive to imaginatively produce in his own consciousness. But what kind of use of the imagination is involved in striving to make present the archetype in consciousness?

In order to lead to the discussion of this peculiar role of the imagination Kant starts by considering a simpler case. He contrasts the presentation of the rational idea in the ideal with the formation of an imaginative standard for what he calls the normal idea, the imaginative presentation of the type or genus. The latter is produced by a superposition of different perceptions retained by the imagination (which in Kant includes what we would call memory), thus resulting in the increased visibility of certain features and the disappearance of others. It is, so to speak, an imaginative averaging, akin to what, later on, Francis Galton attempted by means of photography. The procedure through which Kant describes the formation of the type is clearly of a psychological nature. It is only empirical and cannot serve to account for the constitution of the ideal, the archetype of taste.

Kant gives a further, more interesting reason to explain why the ideal is not made present through such summing up of external manifestations by the reproductive imagination. The normal or average is precisely not expressive of inner qualities: "It will be found that a perfectly regular face . . . ordinarily conveys nothing. This is because it is devoid of anything characteristic, and so the idea of the race is expressed in it rather than the specific qualities of a person" (5:235, footnote). But the opposite of averaging, namely, simple exaggeration, would not do either. The mere exaggeration of certain features would, as Kant points out, merely produce caricature. This is true whether we speak of physiognomic features or mental qualities. The emphasis on one dominant trait of character too easily becomes a subject matter for comedy.

Involving the register of expression in the constitution of the ideal raises a number of further questions. For one thing, expression *(Ausdruck)* is not nearly as central a notion in Kant's account of the judgment upon the beautiful as is for instance the free play of the faculties. Yet, the 'Third Critique' might provide a framework for judgments of physiognomy and expression. Think how a face, for instance, can express a single state of mind (say, sadness) by way of the alignment of its various features. Conversely, eyes are sad not in themselves but only in a face that expresses sadness in their relation to its other traits. The state of mind expressed would then be conceived as the purposive whole whose heterogeneous traits depend on each other in order to produce its expression. But putting it this way precisely brings out the tension between the register of the expressive and that of the aesthetic judgment upon beauty.[5] In subordinating everything to the expression of the single unified state of mind, such judgments would be too close to the presentation of objective finality. The free play of the faculties on the other hand involves a movement of the mind without a purpose. Expressive power seems to go against reflective freedom.

So as to bring together judgment of reflection and judgment of expression, we need to take a detour through another part of Kant's aesthetics. Expression and the movement of the faculties come together in Kant's characterization of the spirituality or soulfulness of great art, that art which is the product of genius. Genius "displays itself, not so much in the working out of the projected end in the presentation of a definite *concept*, as rather in the portrayal or expression of *aesthetic ideas* containing a wealth of material for effecting that intention" (5:317). Just as there is for Kant a systematic unity of concepts under a rational idea, there is a characterization of a dynamic unity in the movement of the mind in judging an aesthetic idea. As we already noted earlier, an aesthetic idea is the converse of a rational idea: Whereas the first is a concept of reason to which no intuition is adequate, the latter is a product of the imagination which no concept can fully capture. But just for that reason, aesthetic ideas can serve to make intuitive rational ideas. Aesthetic ideas "strain after something lying beyond the confines of experience, and so seek to approximate to a presentation of rational concepts (i.e. intellectual ideas) thus giving to these concepts the semblance of an objective reality."[6] It is on this basis that Kant reformulates his understanding of beauty and writes that it "may in general be termed the *expression* of aesthetic ideas" (5:320).

Thus, Kant introduces expression into his account of aesthetics not primarily in order to account for the connection of an inner state and an external manifestation in human physiognomy but rather where there is an essential gap between sensuous presentation and that which is presented, namely, when what is at issue is the presentation of an idea. Expression is not involved in the restful opening of form but rather in the striving of the mind to provide a phenomenal presentation for an idea of reason. With this in mind, Kant's claim that only the expression of the moral in the human figure can be the ideal of beauty appears in a more interesting light. Or at least one might start seeing why it is not a simple imposition of his moral theory on his aesthetics. For, starting from the broader use of the term 'expression' in Kant's aesthetic, one could imagine a variety of contents that could serve in aesthetic ideas. The materials that would be united by such movement, striving to provide an intuitive presentation of ideas of reason, are not limited in advance to what we think of as the expressivity of the human figure. It thus becomes a *real question* in relation to which of these contents or materials we can conceive of an ideal, that is, of a maximum of expression.

Kant would claim that nowhere can we conceive of establishing a maximum in the vigorous movement of the mind to which no concept can be adequate, but in relation to that being who has the idea of reason as his own inner purpose. Only with respect to the human being can we have specificity in the movement of the mind striving to express that inner purpose to allow us to imagine a maximum, yet at the same time retain enough freedom for the imagination, enough distance from a criterially determined state of phenomenal experience.

But, even if we understand better why only the human figure expressing the moral can be a candidate to serve as an ideal for beauty, it is still
not clear how we are to make that standard present to ourselves, for the
preceding considerations might even further complicate its attainment.
The aesthetic idea involves an extreme animation of the mind, a rich and
constant opening of meaning. It is that animation that would provide for
the sense of movement toward the rational idea. But for that very reason it
is an obstacle to the presentation of the ideal. It provokes enthusiasm but
would thereby lack the fixity and unchanging character of the ideal.[7] We
can't quite adopt in this case a scheme of movement toward the ideal. Indeed, what constitutes our understanding of the regulative character of the
idea in the case of knowledge hardly makes sense when we speak of endlessly approaching an ideal of the imagination. For precisely the movement of the imagination toward the idea is the source of the indetermi-
nacy in the object. So, what kind of use of the imagination is involved in
striving to make present the archetype in consciousness? Wouldn't the
archetype itself have to be present to mind in order to beget an imaginative prototype that imitates it? Wouldn't we have to assume the very intuitive manifestation that we strive to beget to be already given for us to
imitate? Yet, the ideal itself is not, strictly speaking, present in intuition.
So, what would count as a sensible imitation of that which, in itself, must
be considered essentially invisible? What is, to put it maybe a bit paradoxically, invisible beauty? We might resign ourselves to gesture, as Kant
does in the 'First Critique,' to the mysterious working of the productive
imagination. But I think that more can be said, even at the risk of specu-
latively extending Kant's own formulations.

I want to return briefly to Kant's account of the transcendental ideal of
knowledge in the 'First Critique.' The singular concretization of the idea
in a maximum of content is God understood as the utmost reality (*omni-
tudo realitatis*). Kant characterizes such an ideal by means of a series of
considerations regarding the nature of negation and the distinction between logical negation, transcendental negation, and limitation. Consider
first the characterization of a maximum in relation to knowledge in terms
of the possibility of ascertaining, with respect to every predicate, whether it
or its negation holds of the object. Such characterization would be wholly

abstract and leave no possibility for having the ideal play a role, even a regulative one in knowledge. This is why Kant moves to consider what he calls 'transcendental negation.'[8] Transcendental negation is privative in relation to a substantive reality. What actually exists would be seen against a horizon of real possibility as a restriction of that fuller reality. To give an example that might clarify the contrast between logical and transcendental negation, if for instance I think in terms of logical negation and determine an object, say, a ball, with respect to its color as red, then in order to characterize completely reality, I would have to assert, in addition to 'the ball is red,' also 'the ball is not green' and 'the ball is not blue,' and so on. If, on the other hand, I started with the form of color, or with a unified space of conditions of possibility of color judgment, what holds in fact would appear as mere limitations of this fuller reality given in the schema of color space.

But something more is at issue in understanding the relation of the finite to the maximum reality, to the ideal of knowledge. The structure at play is that of a limitation of a singular totality (as though recognizing something as limited would place it against the world as a whole as its background). The closest model we can have for such limitation is that given by our sense that a part of space is a delimitation *of* the one all-encompassing space given to us as infinite in intuition. Kant indeed points to the analogy between that which for us is only a subjective condition of possibility of experience and the supposed real ground that is the ideal.

It is with this singular sense of limitation that I want now to return to the account of the ideal of beauty and ask whether we can find in it something paralleling the moment of negativity in the presentation of the ideal of knowledge. Consider first the concept of negative correctness, which Kant also calls the merely academically correct. It is understood as what does not contradict the normal idea of beauty of the species. Thus Kant gives as an example for the human species Polycleitus's famous *Doryphorus* and for its bovine companion Myron's cow. But academic correctness is like logical negation: It has no power to relate us to the ideal. Moreover, Kant's criterion for the correctness of the ideal is, as it should be, aesthetic: It is a judgment whose ultimate ground is feeling: "The correctness of . . . an ideal of beauty," he writes, "is proved by the fact that no sensory charm is allowed to be mixed into the satisfaction in its object, while it nevertheless allows a great interest to be taken in it . . ." (5:236). Correctness is manifest by negating sensory charm. Aesthetically speaking, emotion is that state which is incompatible with charm. It involves, like charm, a sensation, but it is the opposite of the sensation produced by charm. Emotion essentially involves a moment of arrest of the vital movement of the mind, "a momentary inhibition followed by a stronger outpouring of the vital force."[9] Translating this inhibition into a moment of the presentation of the ideal would lead us to seek in its estimation a moment of reaching a limit, though not quite an end point. Given that the ideal appears on the background of the vigorous movement of the mind in judging an aesthetic idea, we would here speak of an arresting moment.[10] That arrest, distinct from the restfulness of beauty, would establish an essential discontinuity between the ideal and its imitation in consciousness. The ideal would be unapproachable, yet, I would argue, it is presentable through that very arrest and discontinuity at a distance, so to speak. Whereas the idea is a concept of reason that is ever approachable, the ideal of beauty would be experienced *as* unapproachable. This unapproachability, related to the incompatibility of the ideal with any charm, might also be called the severe or stern character of the ideal.

Presentation by negation is a characteristic of the sublime. One might say that the moment of negation inherent in the sublime is here transformed into the arrest of the movement toward the idea that creates a striking picture, a recognition of the unapproachable primal image—the archetype. But, whereas for Kant the sublime is the presentation of the moral idea strictly negatively, with the ideal of beauty we get a fixed measure of positive content apart from any rule. (Note that both are schematic presentations, thus distinct from the famous, though weaker, claim that beauty is a *symbol* of morality. In that latter case what is at issue is the formal *analogy* between the activity of our faculties involved in the beautiful and features of willing, such as freedom and universality.)

§2. Colors and the Given

Having reached this limit, I would like to swing to the other extreme of beauty and ask about Kant's treatment of what is hardly a matter for beauty or has in it too much matter to be beauty, namely, the experience of color. At issue then is not the opposition of form and content as in the case of the ideal but rather that of form and matter. The problem we face with color is not the collapse of beauty onto a judgment of perfection but rather onto the merely agreeable.

So, we find Kant arguing that

> in painting, sculpture, and in fact in all the formative arts, in architecture and horticulture, so far as fine arts, the design is what is essential. Here it is not what gratifies in sensation but merely what pleases by its form, that is the fundamental prerequisite for taste. The colours which give brilliancy to the sketch are part of the charm. They may no doubt, in their own way, enliven the object for sensation, but make it really worth looking at and beautiful they cannot. (5:225)

In the 'Analytic of the Beautiful,' color appears mostly as a counterexample, as something we might be tempted to call beautiful, but is in fact merely agreeable to the senses. Kant aligns the pleasure in color with the taste of wine, about which one can at most say: "It is agreeable *to me*." "A violet color," he adds, "is to one soft and lovely: to another dull and faded . . ."[11] (5:212). It is possible to explain the initial exclusion of color from the sphere of beauty by reference to Kant's account of the independence of the judgment of taste from any interest in *the real existence* of the object. Real existence is not a concept but rather is given in sensation. Sensation is "the real in perception" (5:148).

The given must be taken up into an articulated space to play a role at all, be it in cognition, desire, or aesthetic judgment. Just as claims to knowledge involve the commitment to a space of reasons, and just as inclination must be taken up into a maxim of action to play a role in the determination of the will, so the real must be taken into the space of reflection to play any role in a judgment of taste. What makes an effect cannot be beautiful, for the effective does not leave room for the free exercise of judgment. The space opened by reflection is what Kant refers to as the purposive form of the object.[12] To judge color to be beautiful demands then distinguishing its charm, "which may enliven the object for sensation," from the pleasure in the reflection on its form. But what could be the form of reflection of color?

From the point of view of physics, no doubt, causality is operative in seeing colors. Yet, in itself the science involved in explaining color vision does
not preclude purposive reflection on color phenomena. Kant even argues
that Euler's view of color as isochronous vibrations of the ether (namely,
their representation in terms of waves rather than according to Newton's
corpuscular theory of light) suggests that there is also a formal dimension
to their recognizable qualitative distinctions in perception.

Now, real existence manifest in sensation as such has a form. In the
'Anticipations of Perception' in the *Critique of Pure Reason* Kant claims
that "in all appearances the real that is an object of sensation has intensive
magnitude, that is a degree" (A166/B207). The specific quality of a sensation is always an empirical matter, but the internal possibility of intensification or decrease in its intensity is something given to us a priori. The
real in sensation as an intensive magnitude has a temporal schema. Color
is one of the examples of such qualities that have an intensive magnitude:
". . . every sensation, consequently every reality in phenomena, however
small it may be, has a degree, that is, an intensive quantity, which may always be lessened. . . . Every color—for example red—has a degree, which,
be it ever so small, is never the smallest . . ." (A169/B211). Yet, as Kant considers the possibility of beauty in color, it is not to this schema of intensification that he turns, but rather he seeks an element of form in the purity
of color:

> Sensations of color . . . are only entitled to be immediately regarded
> as beautiful where . . . they are *pure*. This is a determination which at
> once goes to their form, and it is the only one which these represen-
> tations possess that admits with certainty of being universally com-
> municated. (5:224)

"The purity of a simple mode of sensation," Kant adds, "means that its
uniformity is not disturbed by any foreign sensation. It belongs merely to
the form." One interpretation of this purity of uniform color is suggested by the further distinction Kant makes between simple and composite colors when he argues that ". . . all simple colors are regarded as
beautiful so far as pure. Composite colors have not this advantage, because not being simple there is no standard for estimating whether they
should be called pure" (5:224). I assume that by "simple colors" Kant

means those color elements out of which color space can be spanned (i.e., the primary colors). They are pure precisely since they can be regarded as playing a role in the constitution of the space of possibility of color. With them color can be considered an element of form. In other words such colors are internally related to the unity of color space or are elements of the color schema for any judgment of color. (Indeed, color is one of the most striking examples of an empirical concept for which we can imagine a schematism. The wheel of color is only the most primitive and initial form of representing the possibilities of color schematically.)

Yet, accounting for the purity of color might require more than the reference to primary colors: consider that the wholenesss of color should be distinguished from the mode of unity of an object by way of its subsumption under a concept. The uniformity of color is a unity of intuition, of space. One need not conceive of color as the color of an object, that is, as the contingent property of an otherwise characterized thing. Color can open an expanse without making it an object in space (think of the blue of the sky). A color expanse, moreover, is not imagined as constructed from its parts. Rather like space itself, its parts are limitations of the whole. In contrast, geometrical structure would objectify parts of space.[13] Thus one might further conjecture that pure color would be color that appears dissociated from any object, as though being a space in itself, or making present to us space as such.

Even if one grants the conclusion that color in its dissociation from objects can precisely be the basis of imagining space as a given whole, the question still remains: In what sense is such a schema for the experience of space as an intuitive whole related to judgments of beauty? For it would not be enough to recognize a formal element in color by relating it to the presentation of space as a form of intuition. One has to view it in relation to such form as is characteristic of the aesthetic. The latter is understood in terms of formal *purposiveness*. Yet, for Kant the notion of purposive organization seems to be understood primarily by way of the schema of a unity of the heterogeneous, which cannot be at play in reflecting on the uniformity of color.

Let me suggest a somewhat speculative solution to the dead end we find ourselves in. Fundamental to the idea of purposiveness is the primacy of the idea of the whole to the composition and relation of its parts. In the aesthetic this is possible without the whole being given as a purpose, without the concept of an end. But one can also think of an extreme case in which parts become merely limitations of a prior intuition of the whole. This is characteristic of what Kant calls the intuitive intellect, whose idea underlies both aesthetic and teleological judgments. As Kant himself points out the sense we have of space as a unique and infinite given whole has some resemblance to that mode of understanding.[14] The imagination opened by uniform colored space can from that perspective be considered a pure moment of the aesthetic, of that absolute, intuitive primacy of whole over parts. This peculiar sense of *totality* in color will be further apparent as we move to the next instance of Kant's discussion of color.

In Kant's account of the division between the arts, as he takes as his guideline the kinds of representations involved in aesthetic appreciation, the beauty of colors to be included in the category of the "art of the play of sensations (as external sense impressions)." As opposed to his attempt earlier in the book to incorporate the sensation of color into aesthetics based on the uniformity of color, the present case essentially depends on the change or the "play of a number of sensations."[15] Kant suggests here that despite the inherent multiplicity in the play of sensations, it can be manifest *experientially* as an indefinite whole or totality that has a dominant affection or mood.[16]

This use of the idea of a play of sensations forming an integral whole (5:329) is striking. Indeed, the 'Third Critique' is full of references to play but almost always to the free play of our *faculties* in relation to a given representation. In the present case, the playfulness is in the matter itself. It is the play of sensations. This constitutes a limit in relation to play as well as to the presentation of form: in beauty the form of finality in the object is manifest by the formal finality in the play of our faculties. As was suggested earlier, if one conceives of the revelation of the object's form by way of the formal finality of the activity of the subject's faculties, it is possible to see the play of the faculties in aesthetic judgment as an extension of mimetic behavior. But of all things colors cannot be imitated (at least by us humans). It is as though color expanses absorb us. In other words, one would not be able to appeal with color to the freedom of the imagination that is essential in the paradigmatic cases of the aesthetic judgment. But the colorful could be that dimension through which the world itself manifests the transformative powers of the imagination, its pliancy, and detachment from interest.

This is no doubt one of the reasons that color figures in Kant's account of the intellectual interest in beauty. Whereas the empirical interest in fostering a social spirit is awakened mainly by cultural products, the intellectual interest is directed solely at the presence of beauty in nature, whose very existence hints at *nature* itself having an end to conform to our power of judgment. Since it is the very existence of attunement with nature that is of interest, the simplest cases of natural beauty, verging on mere charms, will be the most significant. Moreover, as opposed to the judgment of taste, which is always singular and is essentially involved with a certain object, we are here interested in the dispersed multiplicity of beautiful things in our surroundings. Such beauties are not topics of conversation in cultivated society. Their appreciation even involves shunning society in which the social joys of beauty always threaten to minister to vanity. And since the interest in the attunement of nature and our faculties is ultimately of a moral nature, that is, an interest in the highest good, the person who thus "betakes himself to the beautiful in nature" is "regarded with veneration"; even Kant writes, "give him credit for a beautiful soul, to which no connoisseur or art collector can lay claim" (5:300).

Kant goes even a step further in relating color and morality and takes nature's charming colorful beings, such as flowers, butterflies, and birds, as well as the whimsical play of light in nature, to constitute "the cipher in which nature speaks to us figuratively in its beautiful forms." In particular for Kant, colors constitute

> as it were a language in which nature speaks to us and which has the semblance of a *higher meaning.* Thus the white color of the lily seems to dispose the mind to ideas of innocence, and the other seven colors, following the series from the red to the violet, similarly to ideas of (1) sublimity, (2) courage, (3) candor, (4) amiability, (5) modesty, (6) constancy, (7) tenderness. (5:302)

Significantly, Kant's reference to a symbolism of color recurs in the section on beauty as the symbol of morality: "even colors are called innocent, modest, soft, because they excite sensations containing something analogous to the consciousness of the state of mind produced by moral judgments" (5:225). An analogy is constituted by taking our form of cognizing one object to serve us to reflect and make manifest another which itself is not given or might even be invisible. In what sense then do colors in nature have a form that can serve to schematize moral estimates?

In Kant's color scheme, colors are assigned to enduring traits of character (innocence, candor, constancy etc.). I take it then that the relation of color to morality is not based on its being symbolic of the universality of the moral law but rather on the analogy color provides for the simplicity of character. Schiller, who follows up on Kant's account of the intellectual interest in the beautiful in nature, argues that what moves us in natural beauties he calls "naïve" is the way they seem to be eternally one with themselves. One might also call this feature of the naïve the self-enclosed, to suggest that it leaves out the beholder. Its preeminent quality is that it defies identification. Color precludes identification not by turning away from us, for it is merely there without being in any way obtrusive. It is by its complete openness that color disarms us by what might be called its candor.

The detachment of color from form recurs in the dialectic of aesthetic judgment. Kant mentions flowers, blossoms, shapes of plants, as well as the elegance of animal formations as pleading eloquently for the realism of aesthetic finality in nature. But he adds:

> beyond all else, the variety and harmony in the array of colors (in the pheasant, in crustacea, in insects, down even to the meanest flower) so pleasing and charming to the eyes, but which, inasmuch as they touch the bare surface and do not even here in any way affect the structure, of these creatures . . . seem to be planned entirely with a view to outward appearance. (5:347)

Colors can thus be separated from what belongs to the internal purposiveness of an organism to seem as if they are there merely *for appearance's sake*. In fact Kant points out that, most often, that which produces color are processes estimated mechanically rather than teleologically. It is quite common to see in nature a chemical or mechanical process leading to formations of matter seemingly made for aesthetic enjoyment. (Crystallization, which is the transition from a liquid to a solid state, would be another clear example.)

I note that in his account of organisms, Kant emphasizes that the principle of teleological judgment has unrestricted scope. Indeed it applies also to those parts of the organism whose growth can be explained chemically or mechanically, for instance, hair, bone, or nails, for "the cause that accumulates it in the proper place must always be estimated teleologically" (5:377). In other words, colors are a limit case in relation to beauty as well as in relation to the teleological judgment. They are hardly incorporated in the form that opens a space for the beautiful and hardly part of the inner order of physical ends. This is precisely why they can play such a central role in our experience of the world.

To clarify, consider that in discussing the distinction between free and dependent beauty, earlier in the 'Analytic of the Beautiful,' Kant is critical of adding ornamentation to what is independently judged beautiful. This offends him, in particular in the tattooing of the human figure "with all manner of flourishes and light but regular lines, as is done by the New Zealanders" (5:230). Similarly, Kant deplores various ways of painting or coloring the human figure which are extrinsic to its form, "such as roucou among the Caribs and cinnabar among the Iroquois" (5:297). But when we enjoy the beauty of colorful feathers and flowers, we relish precisely *that*, the separation of external appearance from teleological organization. That is, there are cases in which coloring does not strike us as going against inner purpose, when it so to speak of itself detaches itself from form. (This is a small, though significant difference from the case of free beauty, in which we completely ignore purpose.)[17]

We are obviously touching with these questions upon the boundary line between the two parts of the 'Third Critique.' I would like therefore in conclusion to look back on colors now from the other side of the divide, from the point of view of teleological judgment: The consideration of extrinsic purposiveness allows Kant to raise the question of what nature is for man when it is considered as a whole, systematically, and man as a natural being is viewed as part of that system. It is not by way of man's mastery of nature to serve his purpose or make his happiness that Kant relates nature as a whole and man, but rather the final end of nature is culture, of which beauty is an essential part. It is in this context that it becomes possible to conceive of beauty itself, whose particular instances in nature cannot be judged according to extrinsic purposes, to be there *for* man, yet not as something for man to use:

> We may regard it as a favor that nature has extended to us, that besides giving us what is useful it has dispensed beauty and charms in such abundance, and for this we may love it, just as we view it with respect because of its immensity and feel ourselves ennobled by such contemplation—just as if nature had erected and decorated its splendid stage with this precise purpose in mind. (5:380)

This moment, where beauty touches upon the sublime, is further elaborated in a striking footnote comparing the use of the term 'favor' in the two parts of the book:

> In the Part on Aesthetics the statement was made: *we regard nature with favor*, because we take a delight in its form that is altogether free (disinterested). . . . But in a teleological judgment . . . we can *regard it as a favor of nature*, that it has been disposed to promote our culture by exhibiting so many beautiful forms. (5:381)

From the point of view of the first part of the Critique we reach with the favoring we extend to color the extreme point in which meaning is found in that which is merely given. From the perspective of the second part of the Critique we might say that it is the "being given" itself that becomes significant. Only that which need not be taken as part of the internal organization of physical ends can be viewed as merely given, as a favor of nature. This sublime beauty of nature, to which color is central, is probably best expressed by the double meaning of the term 'grace.'

Notes

Introduction

1. References to Kant's writing will follow the quote according to the pagination of the Academy edition of his works. The following translations into English were used: *Critique of Pure Reason*, trans. Paul Guyer and Allen Wood (Cambridge: Cambridge University Press, 1998); *Critique of Practical Reason*, trans. Lewis White Beck (New York: Macmillan, 1985); *Critique of Judgment*, trans. James Creed Meredith (Oxford: Oxford University Press, 1952).

2. As Kant observes:

> General logic contains no precepts at all for the power of judgment, and moreover cannot contain them. For since it abstracts from all content of cognition, nothing remains to it but the business of analytically dividing the mere form of cognition into concepts, judgments, and inferences, and thereby achieving formal rules for all use of the understanding. Now if it wanted to show generally how one ought to subsume under them or not, this could not happen except once again through a rule. But just because this is a rule, it would demand another instruction for the power of judgment . . . (A132/B171)

3. It is important not to think of this as a distinction between the theoretical and the practical. Indeed, when Kant speaks of the need for practice, and the experience that comes with conducting actual business, it would be as relevant for judgments in the domain of practical reason as it is for the domain of cognition.

In both cases, general principles need to be applied to the particular conditions at hand, and both require exercising judgment. Notion such as 'exercise' or 'training' precisely stand between theory and practice and belong to the elaboration of judgment as a field of mediation between the two.

4. Although examples are presented as sharpening the power of judgment, they are problematic where they come to replace understanding something in principle. Indeed the example in its particularity is never fully adequate to the concept. And there is always the danger that we will be too dependent on the features of that specific example rather than grasp precisely the concept through general principles:

> For as far as the correctness and precision of the insight of the understanding is concerned, examples more usually do it some damage, since they only seldom adequately fulfill the condition of the rule (as *casus in terminis*) and beyond this often weaken the effort of the understanding to gain sufficient insight into rules in the universal and independently of the particular circumstances of experience, and thus in the end accustom us to use those rules more like formulas than like principles. (A134/B173)

5. Kant's discussion of the schematism has been read in various ways. Maybe the most famous appropriation of this moment is Heidegger's *Kant and the Question of Metaphysics*, which takes Kant's approach to foreshadow his own elaboration of time as the horizon of Being.

6. The relation between feeling and the balancing of the needs of reason is already formulated in Kant's essay "What Is Orientation in Thinking?"

> I orient myself geographically by all the objective data of the sky only by virtue of a subjective ground of distinction [between my right and my left hand]. One can easily guess by analogy that this kind of orientation will be the business of pure reason in directing its use when, starting from known objects of experience, it tries to extend itself beyond all boundaries of experience, finding no object of intuition but merely space for it. For it is then no longer capable of bringing its judgments, in the determination of its own faculty of judgment, under a definite maxim according to objective grounds of knowledge; it can do so only by a subjective ground of distinction. This subjective means which remains is nothing else than the feeling of a need belonging to reason. ("What Is Orientation in Thinking?," in *Kant's Political Writings*, ed. H. Reiss, trans. H. Nisbet [Cambridge: Cambridge University Press, 1991, p. 296].)

7. A footnote to the 'Transcendental Aesthetic' of the *Critique of Pure Reason* makes that clear:

> The Germans are the only people who currently make use of the word "aesthetic" in order to signify what others call the critique of taste. This usage

originated in the abortive attempt made by Baumgarten, that admirable analytical thinker, to bring the critical treatment of the beautiful under rational principles, and so to raise its rules to the rank of a science. But such endeavors are fruitless. The said rules or criteria are, as regards their chief sources, merely empirical and consequently can never serve as determinate *a priori* laws by which our judgment of taste must be directed. On the contrary, our judgment is the proper test of the correctness of the rules. For this reason it is advisable . . . to give up using the name in this sense of critique of taste, and to reserve it for that doctrine of sensibility which is his true science. . . . (A21/B35)

8. Bridging is not the only figure in Kant's elaboration of judgment. We can find, for instance, such figures as the field, the territory, the realm, and the dwelling place, as well as figures of movement such as the play or harmony of the faculties, the quickening or enlargement of a faculty, and the ratio or proportion between the activity of the faculties. Even if one wanted to relegate those figures to mere stylistic aids for comprehension, one is at least required to interpret them seriously and tie them to the more familiar Kantian philosophical terminology.

I. The Analytic of the Beautiful

Epigraph: from *Walter Benjamin: Selected Writings*, vol. 2, ed. Howard Eiland, Michael W. Jennings, and Gary Smith (Cambridge, MA: Harvard University Press, 1999), p. 547.

1. Ideas in this part were originally explored in the following essays: "On Examples, Representatives, Measures, Standards, and the Ideal," in *Reading Cavell*, ed. Alice Crary and Sanford Shieh (London: Routledge, 2006, pp. 204–217); "Meaning and Aesthetic Judgment in Kant," in *Analytic Kantianism*, ed. James Conant, *Philosophical Topics* 34, nos. 1 and 2 (2006): 21–34.

2. Here a word of caution might be necessary: The notion of disinterest might tempt to an association with the register of morality. But for Kant disinterestedness distinguishes the aesthetic from the moral will just as much as from conditioned desire. For in the moral sphere although the determination of the will does not depend on a pregiven interest, it creates one.

3. In discussing this turn of judgment onto itself in relation to the teleological structure of the natural world Kant writes, "Thus judgment, also, is equipped with an *a priori* principle for the possibility of nature, but only in a subjective respect. By means of this it prescribes a law, not to nature (as autonomy) but to itself (as heautonomy), to guide its reflection upon nature" (5:185). Similarly, we might say that the self-guidance of judgment in aesthetics is orientation by way of feeling.

4. This return from the representation to the faculty is precisely what the meaning of the term "reflection" has for Kant in the *Critique of Pure Reason*. Reflection is essential to the very idea of a transcendental investigation insofar as it refers representations to their conditions of possibility in certain faculties:

Reflection (reflexio) does not concern itself with objects themselves with a view to deriving concepts from them directly, but is a state of mind in which we first set ourselves to discover the subjective conditions under which [alone] we are able to arrive at concepts. It is the consciousness of the relation of given representations to our different sources of knowledge; and only by such consciousness can the relation of the sources of knowledge to one another be rightly determined. (A260/B316)

5. Kant writes:

For instance, by a judgment of taste I describe the rose at which I am looking as beautiful. The judgment, on the other hand, resulting from the comparison of a number of singular representations: Roses in general are beautiful, is no longer pronounced as a purely aesthetic judgment, but as a logical judgment founded on one that is aesthetic. (5:215)

6. I note that, along with the doctor and the jurist, Kant gives the example of the statesman when he discusses in the 'First Critique' the necessity to *exercise* judgment and the impossibility of summing up the proper actualization of that capacity as a body of knowledge.

7. There is nevertheless a limit to this capacity to transmute ugliness and make it part of a beautiful whole:

One kind of ugliness alone is incapable of being represented conformably to nature without destroying all aesthetic delight, and consequently artistic beauty, namely, that which excites *disgust*. For, as in this strange sensation which depends purely on the imagination, the object is represented as insisting, as it were, upon our enjoying it, while we still set our face against it, the artificial representation of the object is no longer distinguishable from the nature of the object itself in our sensation, and so it cannot possibly be regarded as beautiful. (5:312)

8. Kant's use of the term "favor" *(Gunst)* to characterize our relation to beauty is further pointing at this openness:

Of all these three kinds of delight [in the agreeable, the beautiful, and the good], that of taste in the beautiful may be said to be the one and only disinterested and *free* delight; for, with it, no interest, whether of sense or reason, extorts approval. And so we may say that delight in [the] three cases mentioned is related to *inclination*, to *favor*, or to *respect*. For *FAVOR* is the only free liking. (5:210)

Favor is opening up without expecting anything in return and without being constrained by something external. Favor goes beyond what one is obligated to do. It is not exacted but freely given.

9. In order to elucidate the notion of form it is possible to consider one of the most important statements of a formalist position in the arts, namely Clement Greenberg's understanding of modernism. Greenberg himself identifies his outlook on modernism as Kantian in its inspiration:

> I identify Modernism with the intensification, almost the exacerbation, of this self-critical tendency that began with the philosopher Kant. Because he was the first to criticize the means itself of criticism, I conceive of Kant as the first real Modernist. The essence of Modernism lies, as I see it, in the use of the characteristic methods of a discipline to criticize the discipline itself—not in order to subvert it, but to entrench it more firmly in its area of competence . . . ("Modernist Painting," in *Art in Theory 1900–2000: An Anthology of Changing Ideas*, ed. Charles Harrison and Paul Wood [Oxford: Blackwell, 1992], pp. 754–755.)

Modernism is thus comparable to a Kantian project of delimitation. This does not mean only the separation of one medium from another but also the revelation by way of criticism of each medium's inner character. Kantian limits are not external boundaries that allow us to freely move within a certain area as long as we do not transgress them. Rather, they are conditions constitutive of the objects of a domain and our possible relation to them.

Critical activity would reveal the conditions of possibility of an artistic practice. Those human conditions or constraints that constitute a certain domain of artistic practice are called the medium. To do the work of criticism in the arts is to relate the work of art back to its conditions of possibility, thereby revealing form, or the medium. Greenberg thus moves from the weaker claim (expounded, for example, in Lessing's *Laocoön*), that the subject matter chosen must be treated with the means and within the limits of the medium in which it is represented, to the stronger claim, that the artwork must at the same time allow a presentation of the nature of the medium itself. In Modernism the medium is ultimately the content of the work.

The turn of art onto its own medium, which is also the prohibition of art to be as it were the servant of independently communicable contents, defines the tendency of art toward form. We can also call this the tendency of art toward the abstract. Yet, the idea of abstraction would be badly misunderstood if it is thought of merely as the lack of any recognizable representations from our everyday surroundings. Abstraction, the presentation of form, is rather the revelation of the conditions of possibility of an artistic practice.

Form is not given before the concrete, prior to its actualization. The medium is revealed or recognized by the criticism of the work of art. This could be said to be Greenberg's interpretation of Kant's notion of the reflective judgment. It distinguishes modernism from a theoretical endeavor which assumes a prior understanding of the essence of art:

> It should be understood that the self-criticism of Modernist art has never been carried on in any but a spontaneous and largely subliminal way. . . . [I]t has been altogether a question of practice, immanent to practice, and never a

topic of theory. . . . Modernist art does not offer theoretical demonstrations. ("Modernist Painting," in *Art in Theory*, p. 759)

On Greenberg's contrast between avant-garde and kitsch, see further endnote 6 to Part II.

10. So, for instance, Kant locates finality in the representation:

> We are thus left with the subjective finality in the representation of an object, exclusive of any end (objective or subjective)—consequently the bare form of finality in the representation whereby an object is *given* to us, so far as we are conscious of it—as that which is alone capable of constituting the delight . . . (5:221)

And he further identifies finality in the movement of the faculties of the subject: "The consciousness of mere formal finality in the play of the cognitive faculties of the Subject attending a representation whereby an object is given is the pleasure itself . . ." (5:222).

11. In Kant's discussion of genius, to which I turn in Part III of this study, examples and natural talent are aligned. For the gift of genius is precisely "bestowed directly from the hand of nature upon each individual," who "needs no more than an example to set the talent of which he is conscious at work on similar lines" (5:309).

12. Though Stanley Cavell's engagement with Kant's philosophy and Kant's legacy is pervasive in his writings, he rarely discusses directly Kant's *Critique of Judgment*. Yet, many themes in his work can be understood as transformations of Kant's grammar of the field of the aesthetic. This is particularly the case given the centrality of representativeness and exemplification in Cavell's moral perfectionism.

In his essay "Aesthetic Problems of Modern Philosophy," Cavell draws a parallel between the mode of investigation of ordinary language as it is exemplified in the practices of Austin and Wittgenstein, and Kant's account of aesthetic judgment: "Kant's 'universal voice' is, with perhaps a slight shift of accent, what we hear recorded in the philosopher's claim about 'what we say'" (*Must We Mean What We Say: A Book of Essays* [Cambridge: Cambridge University Press, 1969], p. 94). The ordinary language philosopher does not report our common use of words. The philosopher's claims about 'what we say' are therefore really an arrogation of the right to speak for others, without any basis in what is in fact generally agreed upon. The force of this practice is in making the ordinary into a field of intelligence, illuminating it as an ultimate standard of significance. The insights it proposes appear surprising, as they unseat our conventional agreements, but at the same time they appear strangely natural as if "a natural ground of our conventions" (*The Claim of Reason: Skepticism, Morality and Tragedy* [Oxford: Oxford University Press, 1979], p. 125).

Cavell further explicates the difference between the investigation of the grammar of ordinary language and the attempt to provide rules for language by reference to Kant's schematism of concepts. He sees Wittgenstein's account of language as constituting a translation of the Kantian project of laying out the conditions of possibilities of experience "so that it speaks not alone of deducing twelve categories of the understanding but of deriving—say schematizing—every word in which we speak together" (*Conditions Handsome and Unhandsome* [Chicago: University of Chicago Press, 1991], p. 39). If there is in Kant an extension of the schematism to account for the projections of the imagination in relation to concepts in general, it will be precisely in the account of judgment in the 'Third Critique.'

Just as in Kant exemplification bears on the field of teaching and learning, in Cavell the issue is not only that of speaking for others, but of bringing the other to speak with me. Exemplification, following and improvisation or free play, are further taken up by Cavell's investigation of the Hollywood remarriage comedies. These are primarily characterized as a "meet and happy conversation." Here too a Kantian inflection exists as Cavell describes this quality of their relationship as "the achievement of purposiveness without purpose" (*Pursuits of Happiness: The Hollywood Comedy of Remarriage* [Cambridge, MA: Harvard University Press, 1984], p. 113). Kant's account of the aesthetic judgment is further echoed when perfectionist friendship is conceived as "the finding of mutual happiness without a concept . . ." (*Conditions Handsome and Unhandsome*, p. 32).

II. The Analytic of the Sublime

Epigraph: Sigmund Freud, "The Uncanny," in *The Standard Edition of the Complete Psychological Works of Sigmund Freud*, vol. 17: *1917–1919*, trans. James Strachey (London: The Hogarth Press, 1955, p. 238 [translation modified]).

1. Ideas in this part were originally explored in my essay "Kant and the Critique of False Sublimity," *Iyyun: The Jerusalem Philosophical Quarterly* 48 (1999): 69–93.

2. Apprehension and comprehension are central in Kant's account of the role of the imagination in the A edition of the transcendental deduction of the 'First Critique.'

3. This sense of infinite divisibility is invoked by Kant earlier on in his account:

nothing can be given in nature, no matter how great we may judge it to be, which, regarded in some other relation, may not be degraded to the level of the infinitely little, and nothing so small which in comparison with some still smaller standard may not for our imagination be enlarged to the greatness of a world. Telescopes have put within our reach an abundance of material to go upon in making the first observation, and microscopes the same in making the second. (5:250)

4. In order to avoid paradoxical conclusions note that Kant's definition of pleasure in section 10 allows for the *same* state to be, from one point of view, painful and, from the other, pleasurable. Since the definition of pleasure depends on the

causality of the representation with respect to the state of the subject, the same representation can, for faculties having different ends, involve different feelings at one and the same time.

5. In his essay "Art and Objecthood" Michael Fried contrasts the modernist's tendency to the presentation of form to the transgression to mere objecthood found in minimalism (which he also calls literalism):

> There is . . . a sharp contrast between the literalist espousal of objecthood—almost, it seems, as an art in its own right—and modernist painting's self-imposed imperative that it defeat or suspend its own objecthood through the medium of shape. In fact, from the perspective of recent modernist painting, the literalist position evinces a sensibility not simply alien but antithetical to its own: as though, from that perspective, the demands of art and the conditions of objecthood were in direct conflict." (M. Fried, "Art and Objecthood," in *Art in Theory*, pp. 152–153)

Minimalism is effective, but therefore allows for no reflection. Yet, it is not such as to simply make us depend on the sensuous given or on the real existence of the object. Rather, the emotion it provokes is problematically close to an aesthetics of the sublime. Though surely the examples that Kant gives of enormous and violent nature appear to be very different from the minimalist object, they both are instances of what lacks form. Instead of being engaging by way of form, they are occasions for the subject to dramatize his bare presence in the world. The minimalist object is thus highly theatrical.

6. In his 1939 essay "Avant-Garde and Kitsch," Clement Greenberg considers the place of kitsch and its relation to avant-garde culture, or modernism, as he understands it. Modernism in general is viewed as a *critical* enterprise which demands each art to justify its existence in its own terms, that is, show its uniqueness by exhibiting what is specific to it. The arts and each art in particular turn onto their own formal conditions or medium, and away from what can be communicated or from subject matter. This turn of art onto itself also means the problematization of art's relation to its public.

The distinction between kitsch and avant-garde can be expressed in terms of the latter's absolute subordination of aesthetic experience to the presentation of the purity of form, understood as the conditions of representation, the medium. Kitsch, in contrast, is the complete subordination of the means of a medium to the satisfying communication. It is in the service of the creation of effect. Kitsch is easily communicable, for it foregoes the task of presenting the conditions that make experience valuable. It thrives on affective identification with the content which is communicated.

Even such a sketchy view of the nature of kitsch in its contrast to avant-garde practice allows us to see the kind of ramifications this category will have, in Greenberg's eyes, for the sphere of politics. Kitsch is produced for easy assimilation and in response to certain imaginary needs: It substitutes affective release for evaluation in judgment. Kitsch speaks to the false consciousness of the masses, satisfying their artificial needs by means of substitutes for culture. Greenberg views kitsch as "another of the inexpensive ways in which totalitarian regimes seek to ingratiate themselves with their subjects" in order to have greater control over them. (Clement Greenberg, *Art and Culture: Critical Essays* [Boston: Beacon Press, 1961], p. 19.)

But while this analysis of the relation of kitsch and politics might be illuminating for certain situations, it is not adequate to account for the phenomenon of the aestheticization of the political that took place around the time that Greenberg wrote his essay. In particular, it cannot account for the peculiar amalgam of kitsch and terror that characterizes that period. It moreover does not explain the aesthetics which fed the enthusiastic adherence of the people to the regime. That is, kitsch, when understood in terms that are parasitic on the experience of beauty, is localized, framed, separated from the consciousness of reality, at most functioning as a sedative and not as a force that can drive one to involvement with a regime that thrives on violence and destruction.

The category of fanaticism is better suited to describe the aestheticization of politics than that of kitsch. Importantly, the sublime experience is not incompatible with visions of destructiveness, suffering, and horror. It can be aroused precisely through the consideration of history in its most catastrophic and chaotic aspects. Kant writes in the *Critique of Judgment:* "War itself . . . has something sublime about it, and gives the nations that carry it on in such a manner a stamp of mind only the more sublime the more numerous the dangers to which they are exposed, and which they are able to meet with fortitude" (5:263). The dual character of the experience thus seems to provide a way to explain the otherwise mysterious possibility of the immediate juxtaposition of elation and terror.

The understanding of fanaticism as a perversion of the sublime further suggests how it can involve a total commitment in action. Kitsch encourages passivity, whereas fanaticism can lead to an unwavering conviction that would disregard ordinary moral commitments. The moral fanatic imagines he can intuit the unconditioned ground of the will. Fanaticism in politics would similarly hold to a sense of totality in the existence of a people and identify it, that is, make it an object of vision, through the intermediate of the figure of the leader. It would be a formation of unity that would bypass the various ways in which political community forms itself gradually, in time, through its institutions, their successes, and their shortcomings. It is thus the immediate and unconditional surrender of one's judgment to the unconditioned will of the leader.

Kant was said to be filled with enthusiasm in the face of the French Revolution despite the terror it generated. But he himself distinguishes enthusiasm from the fixation of fanaticism. Enthusiasm is a passing elation of the mind that is produced by an excessive animation. As Hannah Arendt has emphasized, this enthusiasm is allowed only to the spectator. (H. Arendt, *Lectures on Kant's Political Philosophy* [Chicago: University of Chicago Press, 1982].) It is permissible on the condition of the complete separation of actor and spectator. Crossing that line can lead to actively striving for the destruction and chaos that forms part of that experience. The consequences of such an aesthetic fanaticism for politics are perhaps best captured at the end of Walter Benjamin's essay "The Work of Art in the Age of Its Technological Reproducibility": "'Fiat ars—pereat mundus,' says fascism, expecting from war, as Marinetti admits, the artistic gratification of a sense perception altered by technology. This is evidently the consummation of *l'art pour l'art*. Humankind, which once, in Homer, was an object of contemplation for the Olympian gods, has now become one for itself. Its self-annihilation has reached the point where it can experience its own annihilation as a supreme aesthetic pleasure. *Such is the aestheticizing of politics, as practiced by fascism. Communism replies by politicizing art*" (*Walter Benjamin: Selected Writings*, vol. 4, p. 270).

7. Kant claims that the untutored man flees from the occasion of experiencing the sublime:

> In fact, without the development of moral ideas, that which, thanks to our preparatory culture, we call sublime, merely strikes the untutored man as terrifying. He will see in the evidences which the ravages of nature give her dominion, and in the vast scale of her might compared with which his own is diminished to insignificance, only the misery, peril, and distress that would compass the man who was thrown to its mercy. (5:265)

Are we similarly defending ourselves against the recognition of the true state of our existence in the world? The experience of the sublime is an affective mode of relating to the world as a whole or to reason's capacity to think and act from this perspective. We can therefore say that avoiding that perspective means being absorbed in experience and its objects. We do not permanently have that standpoint precisely by existing in time and relating to facts of experience rather than to the world as a whole. This is no mere weakness or lack of culture. It is our finite human constitution that makes us incapable of withstanding that relation to the supersensible, if only because we exist under conditions of time whereas the experience of the sublime described by Kant is a canceling of these conditions.

III. Nature and Art

Epigraph: Ludwig Wittgenstein: *Culture and Value*, ed. Georg Henrik von Wright, trans. Peter Winch (Oxford: Blackwell, 1998), p. 20.

1. This is to be contrasted to later elaborations of the field of the aesthetic, such as those of Hegel or Heidegger, who put all the weight on art to the exclusion of beauty in nature. Kant was aware, it seems, that part of what is striking about the phenomenon of beauty is precisely that it can be encountered both in nature and in human production.

2. This is not to say that such beauty really was produced by nature for us to enjoy:

> Flowers, blossoms, even the shapes of plants as a whole, the elegance of animal formations of all kinds, unnecessary for the discharge of any function on their part, but chosen as it were with an eye to our taste; and, beyond all else, the

variety and harmony in the array of colours (in the pheasant, in crustacea, in insects, down even to the meanest flowers), so pleasing and charming to the eyes, but which, inasmuch as they touch the bare surface, and do not even here in any way affect the structure of these creatures—a matter which might have a necessary bearing on their internal ends—seem to be planned entirely with a view to outward appearance: all these lend great weight to the mode of explanation which assumes actual ends of nature in favour of our aesthetic judgement. (5:347, translation modified)

We are tempted by these examples to think in realistic terms of aesthetic finality, and to seek the source of their beauty in the workings of nature, but as Kant stresses, "in such an estimate the question does not turn on what nature is, or even on what it is for us in the way of an end, but on how we take it in." (5:350, translation modified). In particular, natural beauty does not exist *for* our contemplation and aesthetic enjoyment, as though beauty is an objective end of nature, but only turns this face to us as we turn to it disinterestedly.

3. Schiller, referring to Kant's discussion of the intellectual interest in beauty, calls this presence of nature the "naïve." Schiller's discussion of the naïve starts from a reflection on our attraction to certain manifestations of nature precisely because it is nature. He argues that what moves us in such natural beings is the way they seem to be eternally one with themselves. Schiller find in this self-sameness a symbol of the ideal to which humanity strives, of a second nature as a harmonious unity of the moral and the natural orders. This self-enclosedness contrasts with the Kantian vision of our present state as one of endless conflict, of the inner duality of the human being, not only having dual citizenship, in the sensuous and intelligible worlds, but thereby feeling expelled or not at home in either world.

Schiller nevertheless tries to extend the presence of naïve nature so that it becomes a dimension of art itself, that is, something which art would constantly seek to remain true to or make manifest. This is done by a gradual movement of the incorporation of naïve or innocent nature as a place within culture. Even in the initial examples which Schiller provides we can see such a wish to internalize nature in culture. Thus he speaks not only of birds, moss-covered stones, and bees but also of the child and the customs of simple folks.

The figure of the child is crucial in this transposition of nature into culture. The child is not viewed in his weakness, as a creature one sentimentally pities, nor in his playfulness (which might be attractive to the grown-ups as symbolizing a respite from the seriousness of life they experience). The child is an object of awe because of his pure potentiality. The child is yet undetermined, and thus can provide a sense of the freedom to realize the highest possibilities of the human.

The child, or the childlike person, can react in ways that show the lack of worldliness, of knowledge of the ways of the world. Such responses can nevertheless, surprisingly, put all artificial refinement to shame (take, as an example, the tale of the emperor's new clothes). Yet Schiller wants not only to consider the naïve of surprise, but also to conceive of a certain ingrained naïveté as a trait of character.

This possibility is best manifested for him not in the figure of the simpleton but in genius. The idea of a natural simplicity is finally extended to the consideration of a common form of life exhibiting best such natural character. This is the existence of the Greeks of antiquity. An important feature of this manifestation of the naïve in the art of the Greeks is, according to Schiller, a thorough avoidance of the subjective expression of emotion, which appears to the modern sensibility so crucial to the character of art. Art true to nature exhibits a dispassionate contemplation of the world.

4. One can also call the self-enclosed aspect of the work of art, after Michael Fried, its absorbed character. If in the first moment of the 'Analytic of the Beautiful' Kant characterized beauty in terms of the disinterest of the judge of taste, here we can see something analogous being formulated from the point of view of the work of art itself. Art should not appear interested in its beholder. It must not turn itself to the outside, to the beholder, but rather appear to be existing for its own sake alone, as nature would be.

5. It is in the early Romantics that one finds the most elaborate understanding of the inner relation of the work of art and the critical practice. The work of art is realized through the intensification of criticism. One could trace this possibility to a tension inherent in the Kantian account. On the one hand, as I argued, Kant is committed to the idea that reflection reveals form. Such form is understood as conditions of possibility of the content reflected upon. But the possibility of endless reflection demand us to conceive of works of art as aesthetic ideas, as oriented to the unconditioned. The combination of these two insights leads to the central idea of romantic criticism, the interpenetration of forms which produces a movement that is to present us with the *idea* of art. Such interpenetration is a condition in which criticism of one medium (say, painting) takes its cues from the conditions of another medium (say, poetry). As opposed to Greenberg's stricture against the blurring of mediumal distinctions, thus his strict formalism, this romantic "chemistry" derives from the tension between form and idea that is inherent in beauty.

6. In the elaboration of the the fourth moment of the 'Analytic of the Beautiful,' a similar tension concerning the natural and artificial emerged in Kant's attempt to relate common sense to the universal voice:

> But does such a common sense in fact exist as a constitutive principle of the possibility of experience, or is it formed for us as a regulative principle by a still higher principle of reason, that for higher ends first seeks to produce in us a common sense? Is taste, in other words, a natural and original faculty, or is it only the idea of one that is artificial and to be acquired by us, so that a judgment of taste, with its demand for universal assent, is but a demand of reason for generating such unanimity . . . ? These are questions which as yet we are neither willing nor in a position to investigate. (5:240)

Common sense is that natural, senselike dimension upon which judgment relies and the universal voice is only an idea, that is, agreement that is to be constituted, strictly speaking, artificially. But we have no way to attribute primacy to any of these sides. It is not that universal agreement is guaranteed by having its basis in preexisting natural common sense, nor is common sense something that is produced by a higher interest of reason to achieve universal agreement. Nature is not fully realized until agreement is articulated, and agreement cannot be fully validated unless it appears natural to us.

7. This understanding of the life of the work of art is central to Walter Benjamin's appropriation of the Kantian turn in aesthetics. See in particular his essay "The Task of the Translator," in *Walter Benjamin: Selected Writings*, vol. 1, pp. 254–255.

8. Kant's account of the empirical interest in the beautiful suggests the dangers involved in the cultivation of sociability by art. He writes that "as taste thus pays homage to inclination however refined, such interest will nevertheless readily fuse also with all inclinations and passions, which in society attain their greatest variety and highest degree, and . . . can but afford a very ambiguous transition from the agreeable to the good" (5:298).

IV. Extremes of Judgment

Epigraph: Friedrich Schlegel, *Philosophical Fragments*, trans. Peter Firchow with foreword by Rodolphe Gasché (Minneapolis: University of Minessota Press, 1991), p. 30.

1. Kant's discussion of the ideal of beauty in section 17 is liable to appear inessential to laying out the grammar of the judgment of taste. Indeed, this extreme of dependent beauty seems to appeal to the notion of perfection, thus belonging to a conception of beauty which Kant himself rejects. But if Kant's discussion of the ideal is supposed to exemplify an improper understanding of aesthetic judgment, analogous, say, to a use of the categories beyond the bounds of experience, why isn't it treated in the dialectic of aesthetic judgment (as is the case with the ideal of knowledge in the *Critique of Pure Reason*)?

2. Goethe opens his essay "The Influence of Modern Philosophy" with the claim, "I had no sense for philosophy in the real meaning of the word" and follows it with the description of various attempts to seize upon the opinions of philosophers

> as if they were objects from which something might be learned. . . . Then the *Critique of Judgment* fell into my hands, and with this book a wonderful period arrived in my life. Here I found my most disparate interests brought together; products of art and nature were dealt with alike, esthetic and teleological judgment illuminated one another. I did not always agree with the author's way of thinking, and occasionally something seemed to be missing, but the main ideas in the book were completely analogous to my earlier work and thought. The inner life of nature and art, their respective effects as they work from within—all this came to clear expression in the book. The products of these two infinitely vast worlds were shown to exist for their own

sake; things found together might be there *for* one another, but not *because* of one another. (Goethe, *The Collected Works*, vol. 12: *Scientific Studies*, ed. and trans. Douglas Miller [Princeton, NJ: Princeton University Press, 1995], p. 29.)

It is Goethe's classical sensibility that best incorporates the Kantian understanding of the ideal as an archetype. This is the case not only in his understanding of art but also in his method for the scientific study of nature. Consider, for instance, Goethe's remark on Kant's notion of the intuitive understanding or the *intellectus archetypus* from a fragment titled "Judgment through Intuitive Perception":

> Why should it not also hold true in the intellectual area that through an intuitive perception of eternally creative nature we may become worthy of participating spiritually in its creative process? Impelled from the start by an inner need, I had striven unconsciously and incessantly toward primal image and prototype, and had even succeeded in building up a method of representing it which conformed to nature. (Goethe, *Scientific Studies*, p. 31)

3. The ideal of virtue in the figure of the sage of the stoics does not serve to judge the compatibility of this or that way of acting with the moral law. Nor is it a system of precepts for the development of virtue. Rather, it presents an order of character as a whole, in relation to which we judge ourselves, primarily by sensing our limitations. Similarly, when Kant speaks of an archetype of moral perfection in the *Religion*, he refers to Christ. Thus the concretion of the idea in an individual being is the primal image of virtuous character, not the example of a certain type of action.

4. This suggests a more general point: For a work of art, essential change is change in meaning, and it occurs primarily through criticism. An absolute standard, a standard for taste itself, should then be, in some sense, intrinsically uncriticizable. This does not mean that it is so good that there is nothing to say against it, but also that there is nothing to say *for* it. Indeed, criticism, properly understood in the Kantian spirit, is internal criticism that opens up the meaning of a work of art. One could imagine that the excellence of a work would precisely be reflected in how it allows its meaning to unfold by acts of criticism (this is something like the Romantics' take on Kant). But precisely for that reason such a work would not answer to the demands of stability and determinacy required of an *ideal* of beauty. If beautiful form is the space of meaning that is covered and revealed by the movement of reflective judgment, it would follow that the necessary uncriticizability of the model must amount to thinking of it in terms of a maximum of meaningful concrete *content* which is nevertheless not determined by previously given concepts.

5. In *Anthropology from a Pragmatic Point of View* Kant writes:

> The peculiarity of a human *form*, which indicates certain inclinations or faculties of the subject being looked at, cannot be understood by description according to concepts but only by illustration and presentation in intuition or by an imitation of it; whereby the human form in general is set out to

judgment according to its varieties, each one of which is supposed to point to a special inner quality of the human being. (*Anthropology from a Pragmatic Point of View*, ed. Robert B. Louden and Manfred Kuehn [Cambridge: Cambridge University Press, 2006], 7:296.)

6. That movement of meaning unfolds through the relatedness of what Kant calls the 'aesthetic attributes.' Attributes become aesthetic in being related through the movement of the mind that strives to express the idea. (They should not be confused therefore with specific aesthetic properties, that is, such properties whose presence make the object beautiful. Kant of course denies that there are aesthetic properties in that latter sense.) "[Aesthetic attributes] do not, like logical attributes, represent what lies in our concepts . . ." Kant writes,

but rather something else—something that gives the imagination an incentive to spread its flight over a whole host of kindred representations that provoke more thought than admits of expression in a concept determined by words. They furnish an *aesthetic idea*, which serves the above rational idea as a substitute for logical presentation, but with the proper function, however, of animating the mind by opening out for it a prospect into a field of kindred representations stretching beyond its ken. (5:315)

7. Put slightly differently, it would not suffice here to appeal only to the creativity of genius, to account for what it takes to beget the archetype in consciousness, not only because genius is rare, a talent bestowed by nature on unique individuals. Even if we each had something of the creative power of genius, it could not have been the only source of our access to the ideal. For genius, as Kant understands it, precisely provides rich material for reflection but is therefore incapable of imposing on that material the required stability for it to serve as an archetype. Genius produces aesthetic ideas, that is, presentations to which no concept can be fully adequate. But for that very reason products of genius contain an essential ambivalence of meaning.

8. He characterizes it as follows:

A transcendental negation . . . signifies non-being in itself, and is opposed to transcendental affirmation, which is a Something, the concept of which in itself already expresses a being, and hence it is called reality. . . . The opposed negation, on the contrary signifies a mere lack. . . . Now no one can think a negation determinately without grounding it on the opposed affirmation. . . . All concepts of negations are thus derivative, and the realities contain the data, the material, so to speak, of the transcendental content, for the possibility and thoroughgoing determination of all things. (A575/B603)

9. In Kant we find emotion to be associated with the register of the sublime: "Sublimity (with which the feeling of emotion is combined), however, requires another standard for judging than that on which taste is grounded, and thus a

pure judgment of taste has neither charm nor emotion, in a word no sensation, as matter of the aesthetic judgment, for its determining ground" (5:226).

10. A significant example of this moment can be found in Goethe's description of the Laocoon group. He does not direct his analysis to exploring the significance of the contained expression of pain on Laocoon's face, which for Winckelmann exemplified the nobility of spirit which the Greeks strove to present in sculpture. He rather conceives of the presentation in terms of the interrelation of the *three* figures. Moreover, he thinks not only in terms of the moment that has the most potential to open the space of the imagination to the whole scope of the action, which Lessing stressed in his response to Winckelmann. Rather, he describes the force of the sculpture in terms of a moment of arrest that is striking or has a petrifying effect on our imagination. It raises the event to another plane altogether. The undulating movements of the snakes can here stand for the serpentine agitation of meaning that is suddenly immobilized. Thus Goethe describes "the sculpture as a frozen lightning bolt, a wave petrified at the very instant it is about to break upon the shore." (Goethe, *Collected Works*, vol. 3: *Essays on Art and Literature*, ed. John Gearey, trans. Ellen and Ernest von Nardroff [Princeton, NJ: Princeton University Press, 1994], p. 18.)

11. In the 'Transcendental Aesthetic' of the *Critique of Pure Reason* Kant is intent on distinguishing the forms of intuition which are necessary conditions of experience from the specific contribution of our sensibility due to the constitution of our sense organs. The latter category includes colors, which, "since they are mere sensations and not intuitions, do not of themselves yield knowledge of any object, least of all any *a priori* knowledge" (B44). Colors are already aligned there with the taste of the senses, that is, with that which is estimated by way of sensations of pleasure or un-pleasure:

> The taste of wine does not belong to the objective determinations of the wine, not even if by the wine as an object we mean the wine as appearance, but to the special constitution of sense in the subject that tastes it. Colors are not properties of the bodies to the intuition of which they are attached, but only modifications of the sense of sight, which is affected in a certain manner by light. . . . Taste and colors are not necessary conditions under which alone objects can be for us objects of the senses. They are connected with the appearances only as effects accidentally added by the particular constitution of the sense organs. Accordingly, they are not *a priori* representations but are grounded in sensation, and, indeed, in the case of taste, even upon feeling (pleasure and pain), as an effect of sensation. Further, no one can have *a priori* a representation of a color or of any taste . . . (A28–29)

We might further get an inkling of Kant's attitude to color from his figurative use of the term, for instance in the A preface of the 'First Critique': ". . . many a book would have been much clearer if it had not been made quite so clear. For the aids to clarity help in the parts but often confuse in the whole, since the reader cannot quickly enough attain a survey of the whole; and all their bright colors paint over and make unrecognizable the articulation or structure of the system, which yet matters most when it comes to judging its unity and soundness" (Axix). See also the following reference to colors in describing the disunity of a self apart from the transcendental synthesis of apperception: "I would have as multicolored, diverse a self as I have representations of which I am conscious" (B134).

12. Opening up color as a space of form should be distinguished from adding color to what is ultimately a matter of design. The form revealed in reflection must be the form of color itself; otherwise, the latter becomes merely an added charm:

> The *charm* of colors, or of the agreeable tones of instruments may be added: but the *design* in the former and the *composition* in the latter constitute the proper object of the pure judgment of taste. To say that the purity alike of colors and of tones, of their variety and contrast seem to contribute to beauty, is by no means to imply that, because in themselves agreeable, they therefore yield an addition to the delight in the form and one on a par with it. (5:225)

13. This is in part why Kant emphasizes that there is no beauty even in regular geometrical figures since the rule of construction in intuition that constitutes them is too manifest in them. In the second part of the Critique Kant raises the possibility of viewing geometrical figures in terms of formal finality; for instance, the circle can be viewed as presenting perspicuously all solutions to a problem. But precisely because of that completeness, it is too clearly related to a rule:

> Now geometrical regular figures, a circle, a square, a cube, and the like, are commonly brought forward by critics of taste as the most simple and unquestionable examples of beauty. And yet the very reason why they are called regular is because the only way of representing them is by looking on them as mere presentations of a determinate concept by which the figure has its rule (according to which alone it is possible) prescribed for it. (5:241)

14. "[Space] has some resemblance to the real ground of which we are in search" (5:408).

15. Kant's argument for a formal dimension in such a case initially rehearses his earlier reference to Euler's account of colors as vibrations of distinct amplitudes. Even if the specific mathematical properties of physics' description of a certain sensation are imperceptible, still the proportional differences of their respective values can have a qualitative correlate in the perception of differences between one color and another. Moreover, we can even speak of the sensed tonality of a totality of color even though the idea of proportionality cannot be extended to the relatedness there is between colors insofar as they all belong to the same totality.

16. This comes close to what Hegel describes in his *Aesthetics* as the *magic of color*. It is the sense of color as "pure appearance of animation" which Hegel associates with masters of sfumato in painting such as that by Leonardo and Correggio:

This magic of the pure appearance of color has in the main only appeared when the substance and spirit of objects has evaporated. . . . Owing to this ideality, this fusion, this hither and thither of reflections and sheens of color, this mutability and fluidity of transitions, there is spread over the whole with the clarity, the brilliance, the depth, the smooth and luscious lighting of colors, a pure appearance of animation . . . (Hegel, *Aesthetics: Lectures on Fine Art*, vol. 2, trans. T. M. Knox [Oxford: Oxford University Press, 1998], p. 848.)

17. Kant, interestingly, does not address the connection between coloring and mating in the animal world (nor for that matter does he in any way investigate the connection between human beauty and eros). Indeed, given this well-known fact, one might wonder whether color should not go into the teleological account of, say, physical ends of nature or organisms. And yet, mating itself is peculiarly situated in the account of purposiveness, for it is according to Kant the single exception that stands in between internal purposiveness and extrinsic purposiveness. "In [the] pair we have what first forms an *organizing* whole, though not an organized whole in a single body" (5:425). Thus here too color is fitting to the ambiguous position of that function which problematizes individuation or is at the same time internally and externally purposive.

Index